THE GRIND

HOW TO START, GROW, MAINTAIN & EARN MORE MONEY WITH YOUR
TWITCH STREAM

JEFFREY JOHNSTON

Library of Congress Cataloguing information available upon request.

Please contact TheGrindGG@gmail.com for wholesale, library, and legal inquiries.

ISBN: 978-1-73144-176-8

ACKNOWLEDGMENTS:

I want to thank my best friend Adam—better known as NovaWar—who's been an incredible friend and business partner for the past eight years. He wasn't always sold on doing this for a living, but he ultimately decided to go down this road with me. Our video, *When Cheese Fails,* really changed our lives, and it wasn't something we ever planned to happen. I'm happy we're still creating content together after so many years, and hopefully, we'll have many more to come. I want to give an extra special thanks to some community members who have really supported me throughout the years. Without you, I wouldn't have the freedom I have today.

In no particular order:
mrmeeyagi, Kamikazejo, Frysiee,sebri00atomik, PanicSwitch, michaeta, Mrmarton,blackjimmycb, Twitchingbouse, szymc1o, Red_Syns, scream5669, Axiom, WallstreetMonster, makeitwayne, Naeli, itzwalter, x1candyman1x, Sarkam, TeamRegime, soma, wishb0ne, taran858, Thefrenchygames, SuicidalZerg, zsasquatch, SlapHappyElf, Tforty187, Standonurlawn, NickNaylor, Nicknero1405, cptDrPepper, Cakezor, melonlord1125, 2Trainzz, SLweed, Tforty187, Hattori, Therminator, bstullkid, AbsMechanik, majorawesome, Retrodre, icewulfie, JinXero, Alexmhi, Tdll13, Chrusker, Urbanslayer89, Kabamountra, Victory96, Amplefire, Hunter1_2, simplyblake92, yenek, Zero_Blod, haru302, bruteox, boshytips, rastvamphunt, shadyfridge, postalpanda, jaytgaming, haru302, chester804, csninja, eparsons112, Jix, MrKrinn, Thelifeofspark, rockgeta1, jetdrata, demideathwing, tforty187, felixgd, yen111, momoyoisbestgirl, skylinesc, red_leader_zala, spidtaz, th3josegaming, memorexxx, azgoro, made2k, agentwyvern, timjero, pro_kamikaza, trueblade48, xenon_slayer, aeolous16, jamjardavies, alarien26, preposterousone, fortybelow, onedavewreckingcrew, mrlymez, zaberith, about81ninjas, bladediris, griefbane, acehighpl, lunetc. Speakerenderwiggin, eldred57, lingboy, bethamamali

It's always difficult naming people, and I'm sure I've missed some, so to those I missed I apologize. Big thank you to all my mods and lifer subscribers and everyone in The FellowShip Of The Bouses. Without you guys, none of this would have been possible. Lastly, I want to all the viewers including the lurkers, for continuing to tune in and support the stream.

CONTENTS

INTRODUCTION

My name is Jeffrey Johnston, but my fans know me as MaximusBlack.

On September 17^{th,} 2011 I quit my day job to live my dream as a full-time gamer. Since then, I've accumulated over 250,000 YouTube subscribers, 200,000 followers on Twitch, and am safely taking in a six-figure income. Over the past eight years, I've fielded thousands of questions from friends, family, and followers asking things like, "How do you become a professional gamer? What does it take? Where do you start? How do you make money?" I have always enjoyed explaining the industry to people because it's something I love, and it's one of the few things I consider myself to be an expert on. In this book, I'm going to pull back the curtain and share the secrets and tips you need to be successful in the highly competitive market of streaming video games.

I'm going to assume you're reading this book because you're considering starting a stream, or perhaps you've already started the process and aren't getting the results you were hoping for, or maybe you're already a successful streamer looking for another streamer's perspective on the obstacles you face along the way.

As MaximusBlack, I played on three professional Starcraft 2 teams. I started with Check 6 gaming, Quantic Gaming, and It's Gosu. I've traveled around the world and competed at many events and even made it to the main stage of Major League Gaming Anaheim 2013. Go ahead and Google "MaximusBlack MLG 2013" and you'll see my black ass nearly shitting myself from how nervous I was. Throughout this book, you'll learn all about my successes and failures along the way.

You're going to get the information you need from someone who's actually living it. Some of the topics we'll cover include:

- Where to stream

- How to get a Twitch partnership

- What equipment to use

- How to manage expectations and your time

- Branding and networking

- Ways to make money and monetize your channel

- The importance of your health as a streamer

- The mindset of an entrepreneur

- And much more along the way.

You will not find a more informative and honest look inside the streaming world than this book. I'm not going to sugarcoat anything, and I'm not going to just regurgitate information you could find by Googling. My goal is to give you a full understanding of what you're getting yourself into, what you have to look forward to, and most importantly, what tools you need to reach your personal streaming goals.

Alright, let's play.

CHAPTER 1

SETTING UP SHOP

Before deciding which streaming site you're going to game on, or even what games you're going to play, you need to get ahold of the right equipment and software. This means deciding on streaming software, a computer, a microphone, and perhaps a webcam. I'm not going to spend too much time talking about these choices because this is where a lot of aspiring streamers make their first and often fatal mistake: <u>THEY SPEND TOO MUCH TIME SETTING UP.</u>

It's a case of the good ol' analysis paralysis. If you're just starting out, you need to actually get started, and the only way to is to get on The Grind, and press that <u>*GO LIVE*</u> button. Fine-tuning stream settings, logos, donation pop-ups, artwork, and so on will come in time. No point in spending days or weeks trying to perfect the look of your stream when you haven't even started yet. There's a 99% chance that the vision for your stream will change as you start to discover the type of content provider you are.

I can't overstate this: it doesn't have to be perfect from day one. I have changed the look and feel of my stream half a dozen times from the time I started. Now, I'm not telling you to slap together a half-assed looking stream. I'm saying don't obsess over it, don't overthink it. There's no need to try and be on the level of the biggest streamers in the world when you're just starting out. To be frank, some of the biggest streamers in the world have lackluster quality and they still do very well. The reality is, it's not a necessity, but more of a bonus.

Most viewers aren't interested in how nice your artwork is, or how great of a bio you have, they care that your video is in HD and that your microphone doesn't sound like a bag of smashed assholes. If you have those two things covered then you're already off a great start!

The Software

The first and simplest part of the equation is your streaming software. Open Broadcast Software (OBS) is free to download and easy to use. OBS is used by the majority of streamers to broadcast their stream to a streaming platform like Twitch.

Instead of me going into detail in this book about OBS and how it works, I'll have educational videos & tutorials on my website, www.TheGrind.gg. You can think of this site as the companion to this book, and refer to it for software links, information, and direct Amazon links to the hardware you may want to consider buying, such as computer parts, microphones, webcams, peripherals, and so on.

The Computer

The most complicated part of setting up is your hardware choices. It's important you ask yourself several questions: How much money should I spend on a computer? What kind of microphone do I need? The answers depend on how high-quality of a stream you want to provide.

Starting fresh with no hardware could run you anywhere from $1,000 to $3,000, depending on how crazy you want to get, and if you're buying equipment new or used. Chances are if you're planning on streaming PC games over console games, then you likely already have a decent computer to stream from.

My rule of thumb is: you want to be able to stream in at least 720p resolution preferably at 60 frames, but 30 frames per second is fine. I personally stream 720p at 60 frames, and I've never had a complaint from a viewer. Anything above that is just adding a better viewing experience for the viewer, and that's never a bad thing. Most computers at big box retailers like Best Buy have the power to stream at 720p, so don't worry because in most cases you don't have to build some crazy custom gaming machine unless you want to play graphically intensive games at maximum settings.

The Microphone

After a great computer, the second most important piece of hardware is your microphone. If you're just starting out and you're on a budget, a Blue Yeti or AT2020 are great choices. I personally started with a Blue Snowball, eventually upgrading to the AT4040, and now I have a very expensive Neumann TLM103. Depending on your room's sound treatment, you're going to have to choose between two different types of microphones. The first option is a condenser microphone. Condenser microphones are very sensitive and pick up room noise easily. If you're streaming in a carpeted room or a room that doesn't bounce a lot of sound around, then a condenser mic should be fine. The second option is a dynamic microphone., Unlike the condenser microphone, dynamic mics aren't as room sensitive and are designed to only pick sound that's directly being spoken into the microphone. If you're streaming in a small room where sound echoes, or where you can hear street noise or noise coming from other parts of your home, then a dynamic microphone would be a much better choice for you. This is why almost all podcasts use dynamic microphones: if audio levels are set correctly you won't pick up any unwanted noise, within reason of course. The Shure SM7B is the gold standard for dynamic microphones but there are certainly cheaper options. You can find a list of microphones you can choose from on my website www.TheGrind.gg. It's very important that before you try and grow your stream, you have professional video and audio.

Webcam or Not!

The final detail you want to figure out is if you'll be using a webcam or not. Having a webcam is a huge asset. Not only does it give your viewer a face to your voice, but also allows them to see your reactions to what's happening in the game. Using a webcam can create more hype and generate more income for you, but more importantly it will help you create a stronger connection with your viewers. It makes the stream much more personal and allows the viewer to identify more with you. Now, there are a few massive streamers that don't have a webcam, so if you're not comfortable showing your face, that's okay! It will no doubt make it tougher to grow faster, but it can be done. Normally, streamers that don't use webcams are extremely good at the game they play, so they can let their gameplay be the focus. I'm a firm believer that with how saturated and competitive the Twitch market is, you should opt to take advantage of every tool you can. Using a webcam can be a major asset to your stream.

What are Your Stream Goals?

Now that you have your hardware in order and the proper software installed, it's time for you to have a real, no-bullshit talk with yourself about your goals.

Typically, there are three types of streaming goals:

1. **To live the dream as a full-time gamer:** This means you can quit your day job—or maybe put a pause on post-secondary education like I did—and go full-time.
2. **To go part-time as a streamer:** This means you're streaming maybe fifteen to twenty hours a week and making some money gaming while working a day job. Or, perhaps you're a stay-at-home mom or dad that can't commit to gaming 40+ hours a week. You might also simply have no desire to be playing video games and streaming on a full-time basis.
3. **To stream as a hobby:** This is typically a streamer that will boot up his or her stream sometimes after work or school. Pretty much streams when they feel like it. They don't have any real desire or concern to grow and gain an audience, if people show up to watch them great but if not, it doesn't matter. They're just there to have some fun and burn some time. They're normally not overly concerned about branding or overall quality of their stream as the people watching them are mostly friends they know in real life.

To help you decide which of these three goals is most appropriate for you, let me tell you my mindset and how I went from being a hobbyist to a full-time streamer.

My Start

In 2010, I was just getting back on my feet. I worked at a chicken joint as a server waiting tables. I was a 22-year-old university dropout with no real direction or motivation. Even though I was really only barely getting by financially, I finally had some structure in my life. A few years prior I was living in my best-friend Wayne's walk-in closet sleeping on an air mattress for the better part of nine months, all while pissing away my student loan money on partying. I hated school. I hated waking up at 7 am to go to an 8 am economics class I didn't give a shit about. The only thing I knew was that I wanted to own my own business. More specifically, I wanted to move to Montreal and own a chain of donair shops. I thought because Montreal didn't have the iconic East Coast style donairs that it would be a great idea to bring the East Coast flavor there. I even wrote a huge paper and business model in one of my classes that my professor liked. Unfortunately—or fortunately depending on how you look at it—I didn't follow through with these plans. I woke up one morning deep into my second semester of my first year at business school and decided I was done. I just didn't want to be there.

I originally went to university because I thought that's what *normal* people do when they graduate high school. You get a post-secondary education, land a nice paying job, get married, and raise a family. I was so sold on that idea that one year after graduating high school, I re-enrolled to upgrade some of my courses and grades to get a better scholarship because my parents couldn't afford to send me to university. I received a $7,500 scholarship and blew the money on partying and the odd textbook. I ran out of cash and started working at a local movie theater where I met Wayne. He let me sleep in his closet while I got back on my feet in exchange for an endless stream of "coming out of the closet" jokes (believe it or not, I got laid in that closet). I finally got a job working construction and started making decent money. I kept applying to have my own place, but no one wanted to sign me because I had bad credit. I didn't pay my student loan or credit card bills; I clearly had no concept of what responsibility was. I ultimately ended up in a rough neighborhood in an apartment complex known for having drug dealers lounging around. My girlfriend (now wife) was always nervous to walk from the bus stop so I would pick her up and walk her to my apartment.

I ended up getting laid off of my construction job four months into my lease and suddenly couldn't pay rent. I remember going to my apartment one day after lunch with a friend and my locks had been changed. I went to the property manager's office and begged them to let me in to get some of my personal belongings. They told me I wouldn't be allowed entry unless I paid my back rent and if I wanted to fight them about it I would have to go to court. I hopped into my 1991 Honda Civic that wasn't even street legal because it was in such rough shape and, with my tail between my legs, asked my mom if I could stay with her. This wasn't an easy thing to do. I had I moved out of the house at seventeen years old because my parents were always fighting, and I thought I was man enough to take care of myself. It was a huge blow to my pride to move into my mom's small apartment and sleep on her sofa. As moms are, she was happy to have me back home, and it was nice to have some kind of support system back in my life.

Fast forward a few years and I have my own place and a steady job at the chicken joint. My life was under control. I was content, but that was a scary thing for me. I started to see my friends from university graduate and get their careers started. On Facebook I saw people going on vacations and getting married, while I was doing nothing but watching everyone else do the things I wanted to do. Thankfully, that was about to change.

My parents never had much, but one thing they always made sure I had was the newest video game for Christmas. I had a modded PlayStation 1 with hundreds of burnt games. Blockbuster Video (rest its soul) was one of my favorite places to be.

I went in one fateful day with my cousin. We had planned to rent Starfox 64, but they were out of copies, so we decided to rent Starcraft 64 (a real-time strategy by Blizzard Entertainment) instead. I begrudgingly took it home but in no time I got hooked! I played the game eight to ten hours a day every day that summer. I loved the game so much that my parents would ground me by simply taking away Starcraft. When I discovered that there was a PC version of the game, I quickly bought it. That's when I had my first taste of online competitive gaming.

Years later, someone posted on their feed that Starcraft 2 was going to be released. Now, I hadn't played Starcraft for at least four years, but I nevertheless got so excited thinking about how cool the new Starcraft was going to be with updated graphics and mechanics. I rushed over my best friend Adam's house (you might know him as NovaWar) and said: "Dude, we should start a YouTube channel." Without much thought he said, "Okay." I asked him, "What are we going to call it?" At the time he was writing game reviews and doing a video series about video game glitches on his Gamespot blog which he called "Life's A Glitch," so he suggested we call the show Life's A Glitch TV or "LAGTV" for short. I loved the name and on that very day, October 28th, 2010 we created the YouTube channel that would change the course of our lives.

Our first video was posted on YouTube on November 1st, 2010 and featured me doing a tutorial of a Starcraft 2 build. I had no idea what I was doing, but people started leaving nice comments. I was hooked on the positive reinforcement I was getting, and for the first time in years, someone was telling me I was doing a good job instead of being a letdown. I became obsessed with making content. Months later we created a video called "When Cheese Fails 101," and that was the video that changed everything. It went viral getting 100,000+ views when all our other videos were getting a couple hundred at best. We ended up signing what we'd later discover was a shitty contract with Machinima (one of the first and largest gamer talent management firms on YouTube) and after five months of making videos we got our first paycheck for $500. I couldn't believe it. I started this YouTube thing as a hobby and money never crossed my mind until I got that first payment. Shortly thereafter I started to stream live on JustinTV (the precursor to TwitchTV) and told my new followers on YouTube to check it out. I had days that I would make up to $100 from streaming alone with just 30–100 viewers - not a bad wage at all for a stream that didn't have a huge number of viewers. After a few months I was starting to make $1,500–$2000 a month from YouTube and streaming. I loved streaming. It was more personal, and you could interact with the viewers live unlike the comment section on YouTube. Even still, I knew how important

YouTube was going to be in gaining new viewership for my stream because, at the time, streaming video games wasn't very popular. It was around this time when I realized the market was about to explode and I wanted to be there when it did. I finally had a vision and a goal of what I wanted my channels to do for me: I wanted to quit my day job and do something I loved full-time. So, I made a plan, set a goal, and worked towards it. Hopefully this book will help you do the same.

Let me start by giving you an example: Let's say Joe is a huge Fortnite fan and he's also pretty damn good at the game. He watches his favorite streamers on twitch bring in huge concurrent viewership numbers and watches them pull in tens of thousands of dollars a month playing the game. Joe thinks to himself, *I'm as good or better than these players I'm watching, and I want to make the money these streamers are making.* So, Joe creates his Twitch page and goes on YouTube to search up videos on how to set up Streamlabs, spending tons of time setting up a complex array of software and monitoring apps.

If you don't know what Streamlabs is, it's a program that is linked to your stream, and it will keep track and notify you when a donation, paid subscription, or follow happens on your channel. I'm going explain how to properly use Streamlabs to generate the most amount of hype and money for your channel in Chapter 5.

But Joe shouldn't start streaming Fortnite because he wants fast money, he should start streaming because he is good, and he loves playing it. This money-making mindset for a new streamer is setting yourself up for disappointment and failure. I'm not saying Joe shouldn't install and have Streamlabs running at some point, but when you're starting out, you should be doing nothing but networking and devoting as much time as you can to actually streaming.

So, you might be thinking, Jeff, if my goal is to be a part-time or a full-time streamer don't I have to think about money because I have bills to pay? That's a good question. The reason I'm telling you to not worry about money is because you don't even have an audience to monetize yet. There is no point in spending time on something you can't take advantage of. You need to grow a fan base before you try and monetize one. Also, when starting out, every hour of streaming matters. You can't afford to be wasting any time doing anything else besides networking and streaming. Being a new streamer is like being an unpaid intern. You need to bust your ass to get the experience first so that, one day, teams will sign you, sponsors will send you products, and fans will subscribe or donate. Any expectations of making money starting out is a waste of time. If you create money expectations too soon, you're likely going to be disappointed and give up. We don't want you to give up before your goals are realized, so minimizing potential mental setbacks is going to help you on your grind. It's great to be ambitious and have monetary goals, but when it comes to starting a stream try and focus on the things that are going to get you an audience and acclaim, but not the money itself. Down the road, you'll be able to turn that audience into revenue streams.

What Game Should You Play?

One of the most important things you need to figure out before you will likely see any sizable growth is picking a game to "main." That means the vast majority of your time streaming will be playing this certain game. You **MUST** pick a game that you not only like playing, but a game that has a big following. The reality for any successful stream is to dedicate themselves to a game and become well known, famous or infamous. Sure, there are some big streamers that you might already follow who play all kinds of new releases, but you need to understand that 99% of them got famous for grinding one game for years. So, when they switch from their main game, they still hold a substantial number of viewers that will follow him or her to whatever game they want with minimal consequences. Streamers that play multiple games on a regular basis are known as variety streamers. If you're a successful variety streamer, you're living the dream."

Let's explore two example scenarios.

Scenario 1:

Let's look at Joe again. He has grown into a big personality in the Fortnite community. Without fail, he gets 5,000 viewers on his streams. Joe notices another Battle Royale game that catches his eye and decides he's going to try it towards the end of his stream after playing Fortnite. After a fun 6-hour stream of Fortnite, he switches over to Realm Royale. He immediately loses about 2,500 viewers. Some of them are mad at him for turning his back on Fortnite, and some are simply not interested in Realm Royale. So, with a few clicks, Joe went from 5,000 viewers to 2,500 viewers. Still, 2,500 people is a really good viewership, and on Realm Royale, he's immediately number one on the browse page because the second highest viewership is 800. Just like that, Joe gains credibility in another game by capitalizing on your success with your "main." From there it's up to Joe to win over any new Realm Royale viewers with his personality or skill set. Joe's viewership can snowball from here if he is picking the right secondary games at the right times. This tactic of hopping on hot new titles to increase viewership is used by most of the popular streamers. Besides, it's nice for streamers to get to take a break from their main once in a while.

Scenario 2:

Let's now pretend that Joe is a League of Legends streamer that isn't as popular and gets 100 concurrent viewers at most. He is interested in playing the new God of War, so he decides after six hours of grinding LoL and getting his viewership up, he's going to switch over to God of War for the rest of the night. As in Scenario 1, there's a group of people that are not interested in God of War so they leave to watch someone else playing LoL instead. Now instead of 100 viewers, Chris has 30 viewers. Sadly, this now puts Chris behind 50 other streams and he is not visible on God of Wars browse page without scrolling down to find him. Not only that but Chris is disappointed and sad that he lost 70% of his normal viewership all because he wanted to have a relaxing night playing something for fun. He also realizes that if he commits to beating God of War, it's going to take at least 40 hours of playing over the next month, and that's likely going to be 40 hours of no growth for his stream. He might not even be able to enjoy God of War because the lower viewership is on his mind and occasionally fans of his tune and ask when he's playing LoL again, or they're passive-aggressively commenting on how low his viewership is. If Joe dedicates the 40 hours to playing God of War, he might also lose paid subscriptions and not get donations while playing.

These two scenarios are intended to show how switching games to increase viewership is all about timing. If you do it while growing your brand in your main game it can be risky so you should strategically time when you play other games for fun and also calculate the risk/reward ratio. You are not forever bound to the main game you pick, but it's important you choose something and stick with it to start the growing process, and perhaps one day you'll make a strategic transition into something else. I'll discuss many types of transitions you'll likely be faced with in Chapter 6.

Quick Notes:

1. Write down your stream goals: Are you hoping to do this full-time? Maybe just part-time after school or work. Or maybe you're just doing it as a hobby with no real long or short-term goals. Remember there is no right or wrong answer; your goals may change in the future and that's okay too.

2. Choose a main game: Make sure it's one you can potentially see yourself playing daily for years.

3. Choose a game that is popular and has long term sustainability: Which means you can't just choose to main a game that is just popular for this week. You need to think are people still going to be playing this for potentially years to come? Is the developer updating the game to keep it fresh? Some games that currently have big communities and potential staying power include Fortnite, League Of Legends, Hearthstone, World Of Warcraft, PUBG, Overwatch, Counterstrike, Dota 2, Starcraft 2, Runescape, Heroes Of The Storm, Minecraft, and many more. You can always look at the top games streamed on Twitch, Mixer, and YouTube Gaming to see what games are normally most watched. You can also check out a game's official Reddit forum to see how active the community is.

CHAPTER 2

STREAMER ARCHETYPES

Every streamer on Twitch, Mixer, YouTube Gaming, and so on falls under one of three types:

1) **The Professional Player:**

The professional player has mastered their game and plays their game at an elite level. This type of streamer might be an introvert and doesn't feel comfortable putting themselves fully out there. More often than not they don't use a webcam and if they do, they aren't interacting with the stream chat the way other streamer types tend to. If they're playing on a pro-team or living in a team house, interacting with chat and building their own brand are usually on the backburner compared to training to win tournaments. There are exceptions, but typically their careers live and die by the game they play.

Professional players are under an extreme amount of pressure to win or place highly so that they can make money for themselves and their team. If they don't win consistently, they could be cut from their team. So, the "Professional Player" type normally can't afford to be interacting as much with his or her community as they really need to focus on improving their skills and winning.

There is nothing wrong with being this streamer type. If you're not an extrovert or you have little to no desire to let people in on your daily life, or you want to just strictly focus on the game you play, then that's ok! Just understand the specific challenges involved with being this streamer type. Ultimately, you typically have to be playing at an elite level to have a successful and long-lasting career.

If you can't wow your viewer with your skill and you're not doing it with your personality, then why would someone watch you in the first place? You need to captivate your audience, so they stay and watch you instead of someone else. There are hundreds if not thousands of streamers that are really really good at a game but get next to no viewers. If you want to wow your viewers strictly as a player, you need to be truly great. You have to be almost godlike. Your plays have to do the talking for you.

I would suggest that even if you fall under the professional player category you slowly try to make connections with your viewers. Even if it means taking five minutes out of your stream to say hi and ask people how they're doing, it can go a long way towards establishing a connection with your fans. Using social media to tell people how your training is going and what events you have coming up is also a surefire way to create connections. I know this may be hard for introverts or people that are extremely shy and non-confrontational, but these small steps will help you maintain your viewership in the long run.

2) The Personality:

I fall under this archetype and so do most streamers that have had long-term success. I want you to think about any one of the streamers you watch. What keeps you coming back to their streams? Is it their skill? Maybe they have a talent like singing or being an artist. Maybe they make you laugh, or you can relate to them in a certain way. It could be their appearance, how they sound, how trolly they can be, or how nice they are. One way or another, you're probably attracted to their stream because of them, not necessarily the game they play. The game they play might have been the gateway to how you discovered them but may not be the reason you continue to tune in to them specifically.

Being a personality type streamer, in my opinion, is the easiest type of streamer to be, simply because you just have to be yourself, or at most a heightened version of yourself. As a personality, you need to find out what works for you and do that over and over again. This is normally not too difficult to discover because your viewers will tell you when they're having a good time, and they'll tell you when they're not. You'll also be able to tell by other metrics such as viewer engagement via chat or viewership duration.

Before I started streaming, I was really into making music. I was a wannabe rapper and occasionally made gaming parodies for fun. I famously made a song called "Suck My D" live on one of my streams, and people loved it. Yes, it was called "Suck My D," and yes, it's as juvenile as it sounds. I made a music video with clips from the video game Skyrim and it went viral. This was a breakthrough for my stream. In the description of the YouTube video, I posted my stream link and tons of people that discovered the music video on Reddit or YouTube ended up on my Twitch channel. I quickly realized singing was helping my stream grow exponentially. I immediately bought an Auto-Tuner and started singing periodically on my stream, mimicking popular artists like T-Pain. I would do these comedic singing performances if I had a spike in viewership from a host, or if another big stream ended and some of those viewers filtered into my stream. Whenever I sang songs, I noticed people in the chat would say I LOVE THIS STREAM. Then I promised people that for every ten new paid subscribers, I would sing a song. Next thing you know I'm getting 10–30 subscribers a day. Which was adding $50–$100 a day in my pocket.

Now I'm not saying you should sing songs to win over new viewers but if you think there's something that you do to create hype or differentiate yourself from other streamers that people are really gravitating towards, then maybe you're onto something, and you should go after it.

I can tell you from experience, and from talking with other personality streamers, that it is far easier to transition into other main games if your core fanbase is there for YOU and not just the game you play. Now, this doesn't mean you won't be affected by a change in games you play, but you will give yourself the best chance for a successful transition. If you're just a professional player that hasn't made a real personal connection with your fanbase you're likely going to rise and fall with your main game. You have to consider the fact that the game you're playing might not always be popular enough to make a living from, so having other options is the smart thing to do.

Now, being a personality streamer doesn't mean you need to sing and dance or have some kinda circus act. It just means you need to show personality and be somewhat approachable/relatable. This could be as simple as sharing things about your life, your upbringing, passions, taste in music, or entertaining opinions. Caring about your community and getting to know your viewers and their interests will go a long way.

If you make a personal connection with them, your fans are way more likely to become paid subscribers, donate, buy your merch, tune in daily, and support changes to your stream. The connection should be genuine and authentic, not something fake or contrived. Your viewers aren't stupid, they know when you're sincere and when you're full of shit. You have to want to open up a little bit and be vulnerable at times. That's what makes us human and relatable. If you're having a bad or a great day, share that with your community. They will totally understand because they also have bad days. If you intend on being a personality streamer, you can't be this robotic player that shows no emotion.

I was on a few professional Starcraft 2 teams, but I wasn't on the teams because I had a shot at winning big tournaments. I was on these teams as a personality, which means my role was to be a spokesperson. I would make content and promote team sponsors. I would do reviews of products that myself and teammates used. The professional players have no interest in promoting products to their fan base. Almost all of the professional players that were on my teams back then are now nowhere to be found. This is because they didn't make a personal connection with their fan base, and so when Starcraft 2's viewership dropped heavily, and teams disbanded or had to make cuts, the pro-players didn't have enough of a personal following to make a successful transition to another game.

My focus is to build a brand, grow an audience, stay relevant, and monetize. I have a connection with my viewers so they're more likely to trust my opinion on a product. I'm going to talk about this more in detail in the dirty Esports money chapter about the importance of gaining that trust from your fan base and how that can turn into serious sponsorship money. It is not out of the norm for a personality streamer to make way more money with half the viewership of a professional player.

3) The Hybrid Streamer:

The hybrid streamer archetype is a mixture of both elite skills mixed with personality. These types of streamers often have the biggest chance of becoming well-known in the game they main. With the right game being played and extreme dedication of grinding hours into their stream, the hybrid type streamer can become very famous and get paid at the highest levels by sponsors and fans. There is a very good chance the highest view count streamer you like to watch is a hybrid type. They not only hook in new viewers because of how amazing they are at the game they main, but they also are really likable and relatable to the viewer. This is the perfect chemistry for a superstar in the making.

Look at someone like Dwayne The Rock Johnson who started his acting career as a personality type entertainer for the WWE, later landing him small movie roles. When he improved his acting chops, he became a hybrid actor. He still is that really loveable and relatable guy but now has the talent to act next to the best in the world which took him to another level in Hollywood. It's very similar in the streaming world. Take Ninja, for example, who had been a streamer for a long a time and has a great personality. Eventually Fortnite comes out, and Ninja becomes the best in the world at playing it while keeping his personality at the forefront. Now he's the biggest gamer in the world. Both The Rock & Ninja were successful as personalities but when they brought their skill to an elite level, they broke through into the hybrid status which turned them into megastars of their industries.

Just because you're a hybrid streamer doesn't mean you're going to be successful, though. You still need to work very hard to gain viewers, and you still need to play a game that will potentially put you in front of thousands of people.

Being a hybrid streamer is very challenging because you need to focus on the game and improve but also focus on your chat and community. Most personality type streamers like myself have a hard time playing at an elite level because I spend some much time interacting with my chat. I personally have a hard time doing both at once. This doesn't mean I'm not good at the game I main, I'm just not the best in the world.

Hybrid streamers don't have to rely on a team to get them sponsorship deals or notoriety. They often have an agent that funnels them sponsorship deals, and thus they get a bigger cut of said deals. Some hybrid streamers are still on professional teams like TSM for example, but many of them will eventually leave a team and stream solo because the team doesn't do much for them anymore. There would be no point for an already very famous streamer to stay under a team that has certain sponsors they need to promote when the streamer can go to the sponsor through an agent and then land huge six or seven-figure deals. Alternatively, when you're signed under a team, any sponsorship needs permission from the team owner to make sure it doesn't conflict with other team sponsors.

Up and coming hybrid streamers with a lot of buzz get signed to huge teams early on in their careers. A hybrid streamer can also be created by a team. For example, they have a young guy or girl that is really talented at Fortnite but doesn't have a big following yet. The team will push this person into the spotlight because they also have a great personality and can represent the team in a positive light. If the streamer steps up to the occasion, they have a great shot at becoming famous. The team uses their brand to help push the personal brand of the streamer to the next level which can turn them into stars and ultimately bring more money in for the team.

You have many more options and opportunities as a hybrid streamer, but it can be very tough to get to that level, and it normally takes time to develop those skills on both sides. I've personally tried to become one of the best at Starcraft 2 and realized when I focused fully on the game it really hurts what I'm good at doing, which is entertaining people. I was honest with myself and decided to stick with what I was good at: playing at a very high level and being funny. Also, when I focused on trying to be the best, I didn't enjoy the game as much, and my attitude on-stream became very negative out of frustration. This made my viewers unable to fully enjoy my stream. I wish I could be a hybrid streamer, but it's not for me, and I'm ok with that. I still do very well being a personality type and so can you!

Quick Notes:

1. Professional Player: A streamer type that focuses mainly on competing at an elite level. Not overly concerned with growing personal brand. Makes most of their money from Pro Teams or prize money.

2. Personality Streamer: A streamer type that focuses on being entertaining and creating personal connections with his or her viewers. Being great at a game certainly helps but doesn't dictate if they are successful or not.

3. Hybrid Streamer: A streamer that plays the game they're known for at an elite level while also being entertaining and creating personal connections with his or her viewers. The best of both worlds but the hardest to achieve.

CHAPTER 3

TWITCH PARTNERSHIPS

Getting set up on Twitch.tv will be your first real step into your new life as a streamer. After you set up your Twitch page you need to work towards one of the two types of partnerships: affiliate and official. If you're just doing this as a hobby, you'll be fine with just an Affiliate Partnership. If you want this to be a part-time or full-time job, you need to start with an Affiliate Partnership and then work towards an Official Partnership.

Affiliate Partnerships

The Twitch Affiliate level of partnership is easy to achieve and is a straightforward way to start your streaming career. If you're just planning to stream casually for fun and you're not in this for a part-time or a full-time gig, you should still work toward an Affiliate Partnership. As an Affiliate, you'll be able to make money in the following three ways:

Paid Subscriptions:

This will allow your viewers to subscribe monthly to your Twitch channel for $4.99, $9.99, and $24.99. This will be a 50/50 split between yourself and Twitch.

Bits:
Bits are Twitch's version of donations. This will allow your viewers to buy bits packages and donate them to you.

Each bit is worth one cent. So, if someone donates 1,000 bits to your stream, you receive $10 USD. You do not receive this money instantly like a PayPal donation. Instead, Twitch will add this amount to the monthly paycheck they send you.

Game Sales:
Affiliates can earn revenue from the sales of games or in-game items on Twitch. If you're streaming a game that is also available for sale through Twitch, then you can earn 5% of every sale.

The requirements for a Twitch Affiliate partnership at the time of this writing are as follows:

- At least 500 total minutes broadcasted in the last 30 days

- At least seven unique broadcast days in the last 30 days

- An average of three concurrent viewers or more over the last 30 days

- At least 50 Followers

Please note that the Affiliate Partnership perks and requirements may have changed by the time you're reading this book. I will post a direct link to the official Affiliate program page on my website.

The hardest part is gaining 50 followers and having a concurrent viewership of three viewers or more. This is where you will have to start networking to get people to your stream.

The first step you should take is to share when you go live with your friends and family on Facebook, or whatever other social media outlets you use most often. If you're one of those people that hate social media or refuse to use it, streaming probably isn't for you. You don't need to post about every part of your life. It's fine if your social media accounts are solely dedicated to updates about your Twitch and YouTube activity so people can at least know when you're live and other pertinent information.

Let all of your friends and family know on Facebook, tell your co-workers or school friends that you're streaming later on and you want them to come to hang out and play some games. For most people, doing this will get them to at least three concurrent viewers per stream and allow them to become an affiliate.

The second thing you can do to fulfill the Affiliate Partnership requirements is authentically engage other small streamers before your own stream begins. About an hour or two before you start your own stream, go hang out in someone else's stream. Choose someone that has a low view count like yourself. Say the game you're going to play is Fortnite. You should search near the bottom of the list of streamers and interact with someone's chat. Strike up a conversation with the streamer and ask questions like, "When did you start streaming? What're your favorite guns to use? Did you play any battle royales before Fortnite?" Just be engaging, and if they naturally ask you if you play, then you can mention you've just started streaming Fortnite yourself. This way, other people on the stream might check you out, including the streamer themselves. However, you should **NEVER** self-promote directly in someone's stream. Don't tell people you're streaming in ten minutes and to come check you out, and don't ask the streamer to host you or to come to visit your stream.

Don't engage in any aggressive or shameless advertisement of your stream in someone else's chat. This is frowned upon and very rude to the streamer. If you make a genuine connection with a streamer and continue to hang out on his or her stream on a regular basis, that just might open up an opportunity for a host down the road or a duo stream.

Naturally, over time, community members will be more inclined to check out your channel because you're making such a positive impact on the community they enjoy. Networking is a slow and steady grind; you cannot expect someone you just met to host you or agree to duo stream with you, just like you can't expect someone you just met at school to invite you over to their house for dinner that same night. Sure, it may happen once in a while, but you shouldn't expect it, nor should you ask. Just put in the groundwork so that when the opportunity happens you can jump on it.

I hear a lot of jealous people say, "Oh, you just got lucky." Well, I'm a firm believer that "luck" is just the byproduct of when preparation meets opportunity. The more time you spend on other people's streams, the more connections you will make. So, the more networking you do, the "luckier" you will become. Also, feel free to send your little bit of viewers over to that other streamer randomly from time to time. That will get their attention, and you will likely get a great reaction from the streamer and their community. It doesn't mean that they will return the favor but it's a nice thing for you to do.

After telling your family and friends, and networking with other streams over a month or two max, you should be able to qualify for an Affiliate Partnership. It's really that easy! I'll also be going through a lot of different networking strategies in Chapter 8. You'll be able to implement those tips to help with the partnership process as well. If you're planning to make streaming a part-time or a full-time job, then an Affiliate Partnership is only the first step. From there, it's time to grind your way to an official Twitch Partnership.

Official Twitch Partnerships:

Getting an Official Twitch Partnership is a major achievement and a clear indication that you have what it takes to make Twitch streaming a part-time or full-time job. If you're currently a Twitch Affiliate and applied for partnership but got denied, don't get discouraged! Many Affiliates have been rejected from the program a half a dozen times or more before getting accepted. I also know quite a few Affiliate streamers making $50,000 USD or more a year. Just know that getting Twitch Partnership may take you months or even years to achieve. Stay focused and keep grinding towards your goals. If you're talented and hard-working enough, you will get the almighty Official Partnership.

Why is it almighty? Being an Official Twitch partner will open up innumerable doors and allows you to earn substantially more money. There are dozens of amazing reaction-clips of streamers getting the email accepting them into the Twitch partnership program. These clips show streamers getting emotional or screaming in excitement because they know that this opportunity just may change their lives. Not only that but they've also been on the grind for months—or maybe even years—to get to this point, so it's a major milestone in their career.

On top of all of the Affiliate Partnership perks, Official Partners also get the following:

Earn Revenue on Ads

You can run commercials while streaming and earn money. Some streamers will run ads every hour so they can earn an hourly wage while streaming. I'll talk about the advantages and disadvantages of running ads during your stream in Chapter 5.

Verified Checkmark

Just like the Twitter verified checkmark, the Twitch Partner's checkmark allows all other viewers and streamers to know that you're an official Twitch Partner. This is a huge networking tool that brings a lot of attention to you while you're in other streamers' chats. This checkmark will make viewers and other streamers curious about your channel, greatly upping the possibility of them checking you out.

Unlock up to 50 Custom Emotes (Emoticons)

As your paid subscriber count goes up, you will unlock more slots for custom Emotes.

Subscriber Badges

Custom anniversary badges for your paid subscribers depending on how long they have been subscribers. There are three, six, nine, and twelve-month badges as well as two, three, four, five, six plus year badges. I currently have subscribers to my channel that are approaching 80 months! Your subscribers love having the badges as it shows off how long they've been supporting you. Every partner should use this great tool to reward your subscribers for their commitment to your channel.)

Custom Cheer Emotes

Partners are able to have custom cheer emotes for bits donations.

Stream Delay

Have the ability to add a stream delay up to fifteen minutes. Stream delay is great to have if you're playing a competitive event live on stream and you don't want someone you're playing against watching your stream to see what you're doing. That's called "Stream Sniping." It's a form of cheating and something many competitive streamers deal with. Also, Poker streamers rely on a stream delay so that other players they're facing can't go to their stream and see his or her hand.

Priority Help from Twitch

You will have priority email help from Twitch. If you have an issue or a concern and need to contact Twitch, your email to them will be answered before any affiliate emails. I often get a response from Twitch within a couple of hours. That's great considering how many streamers there are on the platform.

Priority in Transcoding

Partners have full access to twitch servers for a better connection. Since there are so many streamers live on Twitch at any given moment, sometimes the Twitch streaming servers get stressed out. As a Twitch Partner, you will have full access to all servers with the best connections and the option to stream at a higher bitrate (quality).

VOD Storage for 60 Days

You have up to 60 days to store your VOD's from past streams. A VOD stands for "Video On Demand." Think of this as you recording and saving your favorite TV shows on your DVR (Digital Video Recorder) at home. You'll be able to do the same thing with your past broadcasts.

The requirements for partnerships continue to change. It used to be that you needed a concurrent viewership of 500 or more, but now people are receiving partnerships with only 75 current viewers. This is likely because viewership isn't the only thing Twitch takes into consideration when entering Official Partnerships.

Here's a list of some of the things Twitch takes into consideration:

Stream Schedule

How often do you stream? How long are your streams? Are you consistent?

Average Concurrent Viewership

What is your average viewer count, and is it consistently on the rise? Are you constantly gaining new subscribers and networking to improve your presence?

Type of Content

Are you following the Terms Of Service? Is your stream unique? What games are you playing? Maybe you're a Twitch Poker streamer or an In Real Life (IRL) streamer.

Audio & Video Quality

Do you have professional audio and video quality? Remember, as a partner, you'll be representing Twitch's brand. They need to hold that partnership status to a high standard. This doesn't mean you need a $1,000 audio setup, but you should be clear and easy to watch.

Chat Activity

How active is your chat? This is normally a clear indication on how engaged your community is and how strong of a network you're building.

Entertainment Value

Do you have the ability to entertain your viewers and wow new viewers that discover your channel? Do you have that star quality?

Social Media Following

If you have a big following on another platform like YouTube, sometimes that is enough for Twitch to partner with you right away.

Twitch knows you will bring your followers to their site and that holds a lot of value.

Those are just some of the things that Twitch looks at when you apply, but this doesn't mean you need to have all of these attributes to get partnered. Viewership, stream consistency, and quality are the most important. Remember, Twitch is a business that can offer you the opportunity to make real money, and they only want to partner with people that take this opportunity seriously.

You may get confused as to why another streamer got partnership before you while you have a larger audience than them. I'll be honest, the Official Partnership process isn't as cut and dry as the Affiliate Partnership. Sure, there are certain things that you must have to become a partner, but ultimately it is a case-by-case process. Don't compare your situation to someone else's, just keep working on improving your stream and partnership will come.

If you apply for partnership and get denied, email Twitch back and ask them what you can do to improve before reapplying. They'll be happy to tell you aspects of your channel to work on. This will give you a clear indication on what Twitch wants to see from you in the future before they consider you for partnership.

Now that you understand your partnership goals and expectations, let's dig deeper on how you can improve your stream and earn more money.

Quick Notes:

1. Check your achievement status: Look on your Twitch dashboard under "Achievements" to see how close you are to being able to apply for Affiliate and Partnership status. This is called "Road To Affiliate" & "Road To Partnership." Just because you meet these requirements doesn't mean you're guaranteed a partnership.

2. It takes a village: When starting out, ask your family and friends to watch your stream to help get your concurrent viewership up.

3. Build community: Network by being active in other streams around your size.

4. Be consistent and keep streaming! If you got what it takes, in time, you will get a partnership.

CHAPTER 4

TIME MANAGEMENT

If there is one thing we all have in common, it's that each of us has 24 hours in a day. As a streamer, you need to figure out how many of those hours in a day you're going to dedicate to streaming, how many you're going to dedicate to networking and bookkeeping, and how many you're going to spend doing extracurricular activities. If you've got a four-inch neckbeard and/or a couple of piss jugs under your desk, you need to learn better time management.

No matter if you're looking to make streaming a part-time job or a full-time career, time management is going to aid in your growth not only as a streamer but also in your personal life. Since some streamers may have a significant other, a child, a job outside of streaming, or are finishing school, time management will play a key role in a streamer's success or failure.

In the summer of 2010, when I was streaming Starcraft 2 part-time, I was obsessed with my time management. Everyone out there that has ever waited tables at a restaurant knows the struggles of a split shift. I would go to work from noon until 3 pm, come home for a couple of hours, and then head back to work from 5 pm until 9 pm. Sometimes if work wasn't busy, I would be cut from a shift and wouldn't work at all.

That summer, I was streaming part-time with around 50–200 viewers per stream. On average, I was making $30–$50 in donations for a full day of streaming. If I made $100 in a day, then I would give my next serving shift to another coworker that wanted the hours, and I would stay home and do a 24-hour live stream.

Those 24-hour streams really helped me grow my viewership, and I would make more money in that 24-hour period then I would have serving at the chicken joint.

Most days I would work my afternoon shift, come home and stream for a couple of hours or make a YouTube video then go back to work from 5 pm until 9 pm, then come home and stream until I was damn near falling asleep at the computer. This would get me 40–50 hours of streaming a week while still working about 30 hours a week at my day job. That's right! Between grinding my day job and my part-time streaming gig, I was putting in anywhere from between 70–100 hours a week.

This is the type of dedication you'll need to put in to become successful in this line of work. I didn't get to go out and party with my friends on a Saturday night. I didn't even have much time to see my family as much as I wanted to; my stream became my extended family. Kayla, my girlfriend at the time, who's now my wife, barely got to see me. This certainly caused a strain on our relationship as I was spending more time playing video games than seeing her. She would wake up at 5 am for work and I was just going to bed after a night of streaming. On top of that we lived in a small, two-bedroom apartment with paper thin walls, so she would be kept up by me yelling and singing all hours of the night. She was a trooper though, and she believed in my dreams and never gave me the ultimatum of choosing her or the stream. I finally felt like I had a purpose, and I could see my dreams of being a full-time gamer within reach. I was so used to feeling like a failure, but in my mind, this was my shot, and I was going to see it through no matter the sacrifice or strain it put on my relationship.

Was that the healthiest mindset? Probably not, but I was young and hungry. I'm not saying if your significant other says, "It's me or the games," that you should pick the games, but if it gets to that point—and you value the relationship and want it to work—you need to manage your time so the other person doesn't feel neglected. It might not be fifteen hours of Netflix and chill per week, but you should make dedicated time for that person. This isn't just a problem for streamers, it can be an issue for any entrepreneur starting his or her own business as it requires a lot of time to run and maintain. It does help to have a partner and family that believes in you, but you need to show them you're taking your goals seriously and show them your progress.

If you're not making progress over time, then maybe they do have reason to be concerned. Your spouse, friends, and family have to understand that you're following your dreams and your time will be limited while you're building your business. A strong support system is going to make things a lot easier for you, but understand not everyone is going to be as enthusiastic as you are about playing video games for a living. Don't let the negativity affect you, stay focused and keep grinding. As you become more successful, you will start to see those very same naysayers come to you for advice about how to run a business or curious about how you make a living playing games.

If you're in school, you will need to manage your time to get in as much quality streaming as possible. I don't suggest dropping out of school so you can stream more unless this is an option you have thought out thoroughly and weighed the pros and cons. You also should have a decent-sized following and be making consistent money for months before even entertaining the idea of dropping out of school. Finishing school and having a degree or a trade will give you something to fall back on should you decide to walk away from streaming down the road. Yes, believe it or not, one day you will get tired of gaming full-time. I know school sucks and the thought of playing video games is much more appealing, but you need to be smart. Just manage your time correctly and work a bit harder to finish your education while simultaneously building your stream brand. It doesn't always have to be one or the other; Twitch isn't going anywhere anytime time soon. This isn't a first to market situation like it was for me seven years ago. Stay focused and grind.

In general, if you're planning to make streaming a paying part-time gig you have to make some serious sacrifices.

Here are a few things you may have to consider cutting down on:

- Less hanging out with friends & family
- Less TV

- Less traveling

- Less time for sports or other fun activities you normally do

This doesn't mean you need to cut out some of these things completely, but depending on how much time you're already allocating to them, you might need to cut back. Think of someone who is trying to lose weight, they're going to need to make time to exercise, and they're going to have to cut out a lot of bad foods they normally eat. It doesn't mean they need to deprive themselves fully from treats, but they need to enjoy them in moderation.

As a streamer, you won't always need to make such big sacrifices, but in the beginning stages, it's so important to focus as much time as possible on actually streaming. Later in your career, you will have earned the option to enjoy more traveling, TV time, or extra time with family and friends. In fact, you'll likely be able to enjoy all the things you cut down on in the past even more than most people, as now you are your own boss and you busted your ass to get to the position you're in today. As Dave Ramsey would say, "Live like no one else, so that later on you can live and give like no one else." What he means is make all the sacrifices no one else around you is willing to make now so that later on you can do all the things everyone around you can't. I can tell you from experience this is true. I'm so happy today that I made the tough sacrifices I did seven years ago. I'm able to do the things I want without too much worry. I'm writing a book right now, and it's taking up between two and four hours of my day five days a week. In the past, I would have never been able to dedicate this kind of time for a passion project that might not even make me money. I'm able to do that today because of the sacrifices and hard work I put in over the years.

If you're fortunate enough to be still living at home with your parents and don't have bills to pay, you have the option to stream just about every day all day. If your living circumstances allow it, you should go into an ultra-grind mode, streaming eight to twelve hours a day, six days a week. This will give you a real perspective of how much you'll need to stream as a full-time streamer. You will also figure out pretty quickly if this is something you enjoy doing. Believe it or not, streaming isn't for every video game lover out there.

It takes a lot of self-discipline, endurance, and talent—you also need to enjoy it.

It doesn't matter what type of streamer you are—professional player, personality, or hybrid—they all require a level of talent and dedication. It's up to you to be honest with yourself—after grinding for six months to a year—about whether or not streaming is the right career for you. If you dread booting up your stream after three months of grinding, then chances are you aren't cut out for this. Perhaps a part-time or a hobbyist streamer is something you should consider. There's nothing wrong with streaming only fifteen to twenty hours a week if you're still having fun and maybe even making some money.

Here's a breakdown of my time management as a part-time and then full-time streamer:

Part-Time Streamer with a Job:

- 9 am: Wake up

- 10 am: Edit YouTube videos or live stream

- 12 pm: Leave to serve at the restaurant

- 3 pm: Home on a break from work, record YouTube videos or live stream

- 5 pm: Go back to work at the restaurant

- 10 pm: Live stream for at least 4–6 hours

- 3 or 4 am: Go to bed

I also normally had two full days off a week from my day job, so I would stream 12–24 hours on those days.

Full-Time Streamer:

- 10 am: Wake up

- 11 am: Exercise and run daily errands

- 12 pm: Stream for at least 10–12 hours

- 11 pm+: Record/edit YouTube content.

I would do this six, sometimes seven days a week.

By this point in my career, I was streaming at least 80 hours a week and would often hit north of 90 hours. I did this for five years straight. I was totally obsessed with growing my stream and making as much money as I could to improve my living conditions for myself and my family. This is the mindset you're going to need, but this level of dedication can backfire on your mental and physical health, so it's important to dedicate time for yourself outside of streaming. I will talk more about this important subject in Chapter 9.

Here's what my schedule looks like now:

- 10 am: Wake up

- 11 am – 2 pm: Exercise while listening to audiobooks or podcasts. Work on my side hustles like writing this book, dealing with rental properties, and depending on the day, record some vlogs for YouTube.

- 2 pm: Stream for 8–10 hours

- 10 or 11 pm: Audition for voice acting gigs or spend the night with my wife.

Note: I take at least one day off a week from streaming to spend time with my wife and just take a break from being in front of the camera. On my days off I will do bookkeeping, have meetings or work on other passion projects that don't feel like work. I do a Podcast every Thursday and I enjoy my summer Saturdays at local car shows or going to garage sales looking for retro video games.

As you can tell, in 2018, I'm able to do more extracurricular activities than ever before. I also take at least two vacations to Las Vegas a year for UFC events without the worry of taking time off from my stream. I made very good money streaming over the years and bought several rental properties that I manage myself that will bring long-term wealth after streaming. Yes, my streaming income has been affected greatly because I only stream about 40 hours a week, but even at only 40 hours a week I'm still making six figures a year off my stream. This sort of success can free you up to try out new passions and earn income outside of streaming.

In the next chapter, I'm going to teach you how to maximize the amount of money you can make streaming so that you'll have this freedom, without the worry of losing a few dollars and being scared you can't pay the bills. Building a solid foundation and community is key to making the latter years of your career less stressful as you make more realistic lifestyle changes.

Quick Notes:

1. In order to make this a viable part-time or full-time job, you need to stream the hours of a part-time or a full-time job. This could 15–60+ hours a week.

2. Manage your time so you can still spend some quality time with your spouse, family, and friends.

3. Make the necessary sacrifices to find more time to stream. This could be less TV, less going out on the weekends, less travel, etc.

4. Create a stream schedule if you have to, as this will help keep you accountable.

CHAPTER 5

DIRTY ESPORTS MONEY

Whether you're a brand-new streamer or a veteran to the grind, we all need to make money to continue to do what we love. Even the most successful streamers making millions a year still strive to earn more, and they should. In this chapter, I'm going to break down in detail how to start earning money with Twitch, and if you're already a successful streamer making a decent living, you'll still pick up on a few tips and tricks to maximize your bottom line.

In this chapter, we'll discuss ad revenue, donations, sponsorships, merchandise, and all the opportunities you'll have to get that Dirty Esports Money.

Before I get into the first revenue stream, I want you to understand that IT'S OKAY to make money gaming. I had a streamer friend named Joe who said he made $80,000 a year. He had a big following and got a concurrent viewership between 800–3,000 viewers. I asked him, "Why aren't you making more?" He seemed confused and replied, "I'm happy with how much I make, it's more than enough to live off of."

There was a problem with his answer: Primarily, Joe was settling and not pushing himself to maximize his earnings. He could have been making double the income with some simple changes! When I pressed further, he told me he was scared to have sponsors because he thought his viewers would call him a "sellout."

At the time, I had a concurrent viewership of 500–2,500 viewers and I was making $100,000 a year in sponsorship deals alone. That wasn't including donations, ad-revenue, paid subscriptions and whatever else I could monetize. So, I knew for a fact that Joe could be earning more.

I told Joe, "It's great that you're making more money than you need to live, and that you want to keep all your viewers happy by not having sponsorship ads on your stream, but you're doing yourself a disservice by not making as much money as you can while you can. You're streaming 80 hours a week and have grown a huge fanbase but yet you're not taking advantage of it. Think of a professional football player. The average NFL career length is about 3.3 years. So, a football player should try and <u>MAKE</u> and <u>SAVE</u> as much money as possible in that time, because they won't play forever. It's the same for a streamer; it's very hard for a streamer to get to the level of being able to make a living, let alone have a career for several years. Just because you're making decent money today doesn't mean you will tomorrow."

Since this conversation, Joe started to see the big picture and began to do a lot more one-off sponsorship deals which I'm sure is adding a nice new income stream for his business. The best part of it is, his community size hasn't been negatively impacted because he is selective on what deals he signs and makes sure it's a good fit for his audience.

Making tons of money streaming is fun and totally doable, but you have to make the right decisions, enter into the right partnerships, and be smart about maximizing your profits at every turn. In this chapter, we'll discuss ad revenue, donations, sponsorships, merchandise, and all the opportunities you'll have to get that dirty Esports Money.

Sponsorships: Know Your Worth

I had another friend, I'll call her Kim, who said she was making $120,000 a year and felt like she was crushing it. When she opened up to me about the details of her income and her sponsorships, it was clear to me that she should be breaking $200,000, but her sponsorship deals were undervaluing her. She didn't realize with some tweaks to her stream and some renegotiated deals she could be making so much more cash. She thought she was on top of the world but didn't know other streamers were being paid thousands more a month for doing the same amount of work. No matter if you're an Affiliate streamer or an Official Partner, you need to know your worth.

When I first started streaming, I had no idea what I was worth because I wasn't thinking of my stream as a business. I was just happy to make making a living playing video game. You need to get out of that mindset and start looking at your social media and stream numbers as potential advertising dollars. Everywhere you look, you see ads. It doesn't matter if you're online or on public transportation every single ad you see costs money to be there, and your stream should be no different. You need to think of your stream as real-estate, and depending on how many viewers you have, your stream could be considered prime real-estate and earn top dollar from advertisers. Most of these advertisers want to spend as little as possible and sadly most streamers aren't business savvy enough to advocate for themselves. Most streamers are just pumped to know a headset company wants to partner with them and the streamer often whores themselves out for "free" gear. You need to understand you're giving advertisers access to prime real estate in exchange for products that cost them pennies to make and send you. If you take that deal and you have a concurrent viewership of 200–500 viewers and also have a few thousand followers on your social media, you just gave that company the cheapest avenue to get in front of thousands of people. Not to mention when you're wearing their headset 40 hours a week on stream, naturally people that watch your stream will want to buy the same headset and ask where they can get it. Don't let them use you like a billboard without paying you accordingly.

Do you really think the same company giving you product in exchange for ads could pull off the same deal with a big streamer? Do you think they could pull off the same deal to YouTube or a TV ad? NO, not a chance in hell. So these companies go after as many small or medium sized streamers and offer products and sometimes a small commission for every item sold. Those kickbacks are very small and shouldn't play a key role in making your decision on signing with a company. When a deal is commission only, I run away from it. The company you're partnering with takes no risks on their end and puts all of the pressure on you to sell, sell, sell. This can become a big turn-off for your viewers.

You need to know these key stats before knowing what you should charge for your stream real-estate.

1) How many unique viewers you get per month on your stream:

On Twitch's backend under stats, you will see a how many concurrent and unique viewers you have per month. Your concurrent viewership might be 150 viewers but your unique viewership in 30 days might be 10,000 viewers. That means a sponsor's logo and products could be seen by 10,000 unique viewers per month, even though you might only have 150 viewers at any given time.

2) How many followers you have on all social media outlets:

Keep track of your followers on Twitter, Instagram, Facebook, and YouTube. In most cases, potential sponsors want to know how big your social media following is. The sponsor may ask you to do a certain number of social media posts per month or even do a product review on your YouTube channel. You should know as much as possible about your followers—including their ages, locations, and so on—in order to help advertisers understand your worth and professionalism.

3) How much money you normally make streaming:

I've been offered to do live events at Pax East, Twitch Con, Quake Con, and MLG. I've done hosting gigs, fan signings and sponsored streams at live events. This normally means you need to travel and be away from your stream for days, so you want to make sure they're paying you for your time.

For example, I normally make $200–$500 a day streaming so if I'm asked to travel across the country to do a two-day event, I want to be paid the money I'm missing out on, plus money for them to use my talent. If they're reaching out to me to do an event, it means they value what I bring to the table. The sponsor should also be paying for flights, hotel, and food. You need to realize that your leaving your stream for three to five days hurts you in the short term.

You're going to lose out on subscribers, donations, and new followers.

This is why it's important to know how much money you make on a daily basis while streaming. You need to add that to your daily rate. Even if the event is one you planned on going to anyway, you should always try and get paid for your time before settling for less. You can't get what you don't ask for. Be reasonable, and don't make ridiculous requests, but don't undervalue yourself.

If it's something you're on the fence about and not sure if you really want to do it, then make sure you're getting paid top dollar before agreeing to it. If it feels like work, then make sure you're getting paid like work. If it's just going to be a fun time and a possible networking opportunity, then you might factor that into your asking price and take a lower rate.

In 2015, I went to a Pax East to do a small hosting gig. I was planning on going to Pax East anyway to meet up with friends and get away from streaming for the weekend. The flights, hotel, and tickets to the event were going to cost me $1,200. The company that wanted me to do the job was offering me all of the above plus a $300 appearance fee for my Saturday afternoon. So that means the job was worth $1,500 to me as I was about to spend $1,200 on my own. I took the deal, I would have taken the deal even if they offered no pay because I was planning on going to the event anyway, but now I had my expenses taken care of.

Side note: Always hand out business cards and network your ass off.

When I finally got to Pax East, I took the time each day to hand out business cards to potential sponsors. When I got home one of them emailed me and I signed a year deal worth $42,000. I managed to keep that sponsor for two years before we parted ways. So, always keep in mind that on top of being paid to go to the events and network or represent a company, you also have the opportunity to make new deals there.

What are the Terms?

This is a tough question to answer as every deal is different. There are many factors at play such as:

- How long is the sponsorship term?

- Is it a one-off deal for a couple of days or hours?

- Is it a three or six-month deal?

- Is it a one-year deal?

- What are they asking of you?

- Are they just looking for Twitch promotion?

- Are they asking for social media posts?

- Are they looking for an exclusivity deal so you can't use a competitor's product?

- Are they asking for YouTube reviews?

- Are they able to do anything for you outside of pay? Are they willing to plug your stream on social media and help you grow?

- How expensive are their products that they are supplying you with?

You better not be doing a bunch of work for some cheap $60 product you can buy in the stores. If they're providing you with thousands of dollar's worth of computer equipment or microphones, that's a different story. What they're offering you in product should play a big role in what you ask for in a monthly salary. Remember, commission only deals are garbage unless they're providing you with some really great products.

Is This Actually a Company You Want to be Sponsored By?

Sometimes you will be asked to play a game that you don't think looks very good, and they aren't offering to pay you much money at all. Maybe they offer you some free game keys for your stream and $100 to play the game for two hours. If it isn't a game you think looks great, then it's probably best you just say no.

What if it was the same game, but they were offering to pay you $2,000 for two hours? It's true that some people might label you a sellout, but you need to suck it up, be a professional, and play the game. This is your business and your livelihood. If the game does suck, you don't simply say this game sucks and collect the paycheck. You suggest things that you think would improve the game and also speak nicely about the things they pull off. That way you don't burn a bridge with a high paying client and you're honest to your community about what works and what you think needs work. Getting that nice payday allows you to save up money so that you can continue to stream if and when you have down periods in your business. There is nothing wrong with making money, and don't let random trolls tell you otherwise. As long as it's ethical and in good faith, then do it. The more you make, the longer you get to enjoy this amazing career, never apologize for running a successful business.

How Can Agents Help?

Much like the movie business, medium and high-profile streamers often work with an agent. There are mainly two types of relationships agents have with talent.

1) Exclusive:

This is when a talent signs an exclusivity deal with an agency, which means the talent goes under contract agreeing to not get deals from other agents and they normally can't sign their own personal deals without going through their agency to go over and negotiate the terms for them. These kinds of deals are normally done with mega-streamers that have huge numbers. Agency's fight to get talent to sign with them as they know there are huge commissions to be made. Signing a superstar streamer or the next big thing could literally make an agency and open up lots of doors for them. In case you're still naive about the money to be made in this industry, some streamers sign deals in the realm of millions of dollars. You may have wondered why you see a lot the same people doing live events or the same streamers doing sponsored content on Twitch. It's likely they're all getting the deal from the same agency. That agency gets a lot of work, and they always get their most popular talent to do the job. I personally never signed an exclusivity deal because I'm savvy enough to find my own deals, and I've also created good relationships with agents that don't require exclusivity.

2) Non-Exclusive:

These are types of agents I deal with. I currently get deals from four different agents. Most of the time the deals are one-offs, which means I promote a game for a stream or two, or I go to a live event to host it or take part in it. I prefer to do it this way because it allows me opportunities from many sources instead of just one. I'm also a black male, and many companies need to show diversity in their advertisements. I take pride in my work, so I get a fair amount deals because I always do a good job. In non-exclusive deals, you normally don't get the premium sponsors, but great opportunities do pop up on a regular basis. The best part is you're able to find your own deals on the side yourself, and no one can pitch you better than YOU!

Where Can You Find Gaming Agents?

The easiest way to find gaming agents is to ask other streamers that have sponsorship deals who they deal with. It's important that you're asking streamers that you have a relationship with already. It's also important you don't do it while they're streaming. Emailing them, or private messaging them on Twitter or Facebook will allow the streamer you're asking to reply to you on their own time and you don't put them on the spot. In the message, explain to them you're looking to get sponsors and are seeking representation. Compliment them on the quality of sponsors they have and ask if you could get the contact information of the person they work with. If they provide you with contact information, make sure you tell the agent what streamer sent you. Sometimes talent can get referral bonuses if they bring another client on board.

I myself often act as an agent and get sponsorship deals for streamers big and small. If you're looking for potential sponsorship opportunities through me, go to my website (www.thegrind.gg) and fill out your stream information on the sponsorship page.

How to Find and Contact Sponsors Without an Agent?

Before you reach out to a sponsor, it's important to have all the information I talked about before, such as your social media numbers and stream viewership numbers. You should save all this information in a word document so you can copy and paste them to many different sponsors. Be sure to update this information as your numbers change. If you want to look more professional, you can create a "pitch deck." A pitch deck is a fancy image with all your stats. Here is a section of the pitch deck I use for my Podcast, *Technical Alpha*:

As you can see, this is much more aesthetically pleasing to the eye than some pasted text. It creates a great first impression to the sponsor that you take pride in your work, and it will set you apart from most other streamers. I personally have no artistic ability when it comes to creating things like this, so my YouTube partner NovaWar made this. If you have the talent to make something that looks nice and is easy to read, then go for it! If not, it might be worth it to hire a designer to put something together.

Assuming you have all the critical information that a potential sponsor would like to see, it's now time to reach out and see who takes a bite. There are primarily two main ways you can do this:

1) Go directly to their website and apply for sponsorships. If the company you're going after already sponsors other streamers, then they'll likely have a sponsorship contact page. If they don't, look for the email address of the partnerships or marketing department and shoot them an email.

2) Another good option, and my personal favorite, is Twitter private messaging. Normally a company's Twitter is very active and routinely monitored, so you'll likely get a quick response. If the person on Twitter can't help you, they'll normally give you a direct email contact of the person you should reach out to. Thank them and ask for their name. When you send the email, mention the person's name from Twitter and say they sent you.

Here's a trick I like to do before contacting a sponsor on Twitter. If they sell a product you already use—like a headset—then while you're streaming and at a daily peak viewership, take a screenshot of you wearing the headset and tweet out to them the picture and say something nice like, "My Sennheiser Game One headset sounds amazing, I can hear people coming from a mile away while playing Fortnite!" After you're done tweeting, ask your entire live stream audience to go and retweet and like your tweet. This will get you tons of likes, and it'll get the attention of the company. This is almost like a soft audition; the potential sponsor will immediately see the reach and engagement you have with your community. After your stream, or a day or so later, you can reach out to the company.

This is a great way to do a cold call but back it up with proof that you're worth talking to.

What Do You Say to a Potential Sponsor?

Your first contact with a potential sponsor should be short and to the point. Here's an example of a first contact message I would send:

> Hey there, I'm reaching out in hopes I could speak to someone about a possible sponsorship. I've been using your products for years and my community members keep asking me where they can buy your headsets. I would love to get my hands on your newest headset and show it off to my community. I've been a Twitch streamer for over 7 years and have over 200,000 followers on my social media accounts. It would be a natural and organic partnership as I already use and enjoy your products. I'll drop all my personal links below so you can check me out. I would greatly appreciate an opportunity to speak to someone a bit more in detail on how we could work together in the future. Thank you for your time and look forward to hearing from you soon.
>
> Jeff
> (Then I would add all my social media links.)

It's important you explicitly ask for the opportunity to speak to someone about it because if they're interested, they will tell you who to reach out to. They will also be curious about what kind of partnership deal you're looking for. Before getting on a call with them, it's important to know your stream numbers and be confident in yourself. Never lie about your numbers or overpromise. I could write an entire book about this process, but every deal, every streamer, and every sponsor are different. There are different goals and budgets in every situation. If you want some one-on-one coaching and to help reach out to sponsors, you can sign up for a consultation with me on The Grind website. Hopefully, these tips and tricks will help you land a sponsorship deal.

Don't be afraid to think outside the box; I've gotten sponsorship deals from watch companies, underwear companies, and even fitness gyms. You don't always have to go after sponsors that everyone else has. Go after companies that you enjoy and use on a regular basis. Don't be afraid of rejection, it will happen a lot. Some companies might not like your style of entertainment. It's your job to show them the value you bring to the table and then sell them on it.

Ad-Revenue:

One of the benefits of becoming a Twitch Partner is having the option of running ads on your stream. There is a science when it comes to running ads on stream, and it's important you understand the pros and cons.

When you're watching YouTube videos, and an ad pops up at the start, what is the first thing you look for? Chances are it's the skip ad button because we all hate watching ads. Well, it's the same thing on Twitch: you have to consider that playing ads just might cost you viewers. So, picking the right times to play ads is very important. Here's a list of strategic times to play ads and why:

Bathroom Breaks:
This is a great time to play ads throughout the day because you're away from the computer and the viewer doesn't feel like they're missing out on entertainment. Keep in mind that running ads even while you're away from the computer will likely still cause some viewers to leave, so don't pretend to go to the bathroom every hour to sneak in more ads—your viewers aren't dumb.

In Between Long Game Queues:
For streamers that play games with long queue times between matches, they may opt to play a set of ads during the waiting period. For example, people that play League of Legends are often in games that last 30+ minutes, and they can wait another five to fifteen minutes to get into another game. It's common for streamers to run a set of ads during this lobby wait time. You MUST take into consideration that after a game you might naturally lose viewers as they just wanted to stick around long enough to see the outcome of your last game, so running ads right after a game will only multiply the potential of losing more viewers.

End of the Stream:
This is my personal favorite time to run ads. I know I'm leaving money on the table by not running them throughout the stream, but I'd rather not bombard my community with ads when I don't need to. At the end of your stream you can vocally tell everyone, "Thanks for tuning in, I'll see you the same time tomorrow. Before I log off, I'm going to run some ads, and I'd appreciate it if you stuck around to watch them." You'll be surprised with how many of your loyal viewers will stick around to watch you run three to five minutes of ads. It's a very popular choice for streamers to run ads at the end of the stream. This allows you to make a few dollars and piss off a minimal amount of people in the process.

How Much Will You Make from Running Ads?

On your Twitch dashboard, you will see an approximate dollar amount you will get paid for running a certain number of ads. They calculate this figure using your current viewer count. For example, if you have 100 viewers and you run a two-minute ad, your pay might only be $1.50. If you have 2,000 viewers your pay for running a two-minute ad might be $10. If you have 20,000 viewers your pay might be $100. You need to ask yourself: With only 100 viewers, is earning that $1.50 worth losing 5–10% of your viewership? Remember that every time you play ads, you're likely going to lose viewers. If you lose viewers, that may put you lower on the Twitch directory list for that game, which makes it harder for potential new viewers to find you. If you're already one of the top streamers for the game you're playing, then running ads doesn't negatively affect you as much. However, when you're just starting to grind, you have to make these calculations and decide what your priorities are at any given time.

Keep in mind that ads are worth a lot more during certain times of the year. Typically, around Christmas and the winter holidays—November through December—CPM is at its highest. CPM stands for "Cost Per Mille," which simply means cost per thousand and is the measure by which you are paid for an impression. An impression is someone watching your video for a certain amount of time. For example, say your rate of pay is $5 CPM. This means for every one thousand viewers that see the ad, you would get paid $5.

If 1,000 viewers watched you run five ads at a $5 CPM, you would receive $25. Around the holidays, ad companies are paying top dollar because they know people are in spending mode around Christmas time. I find January to March to be when CPM rates are at yearly lows because companies know people just spent a lot of money on the holidays and are recovering.

The other thing to take into consideration is how much community support you are getting without running ads. I'll use my stream for example. I'm making on average $200–$500 a day from donations and subscriptions, which alleviates the pressure of needing to play ads. I'm already making good money, and so it isn't worth the risk of losing viewers just to make an extra $20 a day in ads. Now, I'm not saying just because you're making good money doesn't mean you shouldn't run ads, but you should consider limiting the number of ads you play or at least run them at down periods of your stream like I discussed earlier.

If you're struggling with getting donations and subscriptions, then you might want to consider running enough ads per day so you can make a decent wage. Some streamers will play enough ads so they make a certain amount of money a day, just like a regular day job. For example, you might get new subscribers and $20 in donations most days, so you make sure to run enough ads to put another $20 in your pocket. The bottom line is everyone's situation is different, and only you can decide if running a little or a lot of ads is right for you.

To me, ad-revenue should just be icing on the cake; you should be getting most of your income from paid subscriptions, donations, and sponsors. The only time I can see ad-revenue being worth more than any of those other revenue streams is if you have thousands or tens of thousands of viewers. Even still, you'll never be exempt from the negative effects of too many ads.

Donations:

Talking about donations and how to earn more of them can be a bit of a taboo subject for streamers. Streamers often don't like talking about how much in donations they make per stream because they fear if the viewers really knew how much they get, then they wouldn't want to keep giving. Some people simply don't want the world to know how much money they earn, and they have that right. I'm going to share some of the tactics that streamers use to get more donations, but before I do I want you to remember what I said earlier: It's is OK to make money as a streamer.

Never apologize for running a successful business. There will be people in your stream that will talk shit about you for making "easy money," when in reality there is nothing easy about it. It takes a lot of sacrifices and commitment to get to the point where you're doing well in the donation department. Ignore the jealous haters in your chat and stay focused on entertaining your audience. Don't let the vocal minority make you feel guilty or stop you from earning more money and supporting yourself and your family.

Depending on the type of streamer you are, donations can be your biggest source of income. Personality and hybrid type streamers often make a killing in donations because they have a connection with their viewers. The stronger the connection with your viewers, the more likely they're going to go above and beyond to make sure you're taken care of. Your supporters want you to succeed, and in many cases they even consider you a friend they have never met. A donation is one of the biggest compliments a viewer can give to you as a streamer. They don't need to give you money, yet they choose to do so. Whether they're donating $5 or $500, you should always be thankful for the kind gesture.

One of the most important things you should know when it comes to upselling your viewers on a subscription, donation, or merchandise, is that they want to spend money on you—you just have to give them a reason to. When I first started streaming, I would on average get about $30–$50 a day in donations and I thought that was incredible. I had a donation button on my stream page, but I never really made donations an entertainment factor, and my reactions to donations at the time were a simple, "Thank you." I've made some serious changes to the way donations are handled on my stream, and it has paid off handsomely. Just yesterday, I had $731 USD in donations after a nine-hour stream. When you convert that to my crappy Canadian pesos that's about $950 CAD! Not bad for a day's work, eh? I know some of you readers are probably thinking *that would never happen to me*, but seeing streamers make this kind of money (or more) isn't out of the norm.

The information I'm about to share is going to make your investment in this book pay off 100 times over. No matter if you currently have twenty viewers or 2,000 viewers, here are some powerful tips and tricks you can start employing to earn more donations on a daily basis.

Giving Proper Recognition:

Every time someone donates you should always thank them by username. This achieves two things. First, it gives the donator a moment in the spotlight, and second; it lets everyone else know that giving donations is a positive way to communicate with you. I'm sure you've noticed as a viewer or a streamer that donations come in waves. That's because it creates a chain effect. When you're reacting to donations, it naturally becomes the focus of the stream and others want to get in on the hype.

The next way to give proper recognition is to have the names of the supporters on the screen. This is the standard practice now among all streamers. This allows the top donators or most recent to have their names on the stream until they are beaten by a bigger or more recent donation. This can often create "Donation Wars" between viewers where they are battling to be the biggest supporter of the day or the month. These donations wars create a lot of hype and are normally fun for the entire stream. I suggest using Streamlabs for all of your donation needs. It's very easy to set up, and the program will automatically update your top and recent donations for you. If you want to learn more about how to set up Streamlabs be sure to go to The Grind website and check out some of my video tutorials.

One thing that may not come naturally is: give bigger reactions to bigger donations. Believe it or not, I see some streamers react the same way for a $10 donation as they do for a $100 donation. If you're going to give off the same reaction for any amount of money, then why should the viewer give a lot? Naturally, you're probably going to go crazy when a $100 donation comes through because when the viewer sends that money, they are all ears awaiting your reaction. If your reaction isn't exciting, then maybe they will think twice about giving that amount again. Remember that your reaction is important to the person giving you money and that is part of their entertainment. Sure, they want to support you, but it's your job to make that person feel good about giving. Positive reactions are infectious...so be infectious!

When watching a huge streamer, you might notice they have donations coming in every other minute without any time to thank every person. But when they get a big donation, they make an immediate and commensurate reaction. Every donation is important and something to be grateful for, but let's be real—bigger donations deserve bigger reactions.

When I get a big donation, I often improvise a song about the donor. If it's a massive donation, I'll put on full chain mail and sing Master Exploder by Tenacious D. This puts a smile on everyone's face and often times wins new viewers in the process.

Here's me in action after a huge donation

This doesn't mean you have to sing songs or act as crazy as I do, just come up with your own thing. Some artists will draw a portrait or a character for big donations. Some streamers will play games with big donors to give more value. Whatever you decide to do, just make sure it comes from the heart, and your reactions are genuine and authentic.

Donation Popups:

Through Streamlabs you can create unique gif pop-ups and sounds for certain donation amounts. This has also become a standard among almost all streamers. The real magic comes from what sounds and gifs you're using. You want to choose sounds and popups that cater to your stream. Let's say you're a huge Pokémon fan. Maybe your $5 donation alert is the sound of your favorite Pokémon, and a gif of that Pokémon pops up on screen. Personally, I love playing horror games, and I get scared easily while playing them alone in the dark. My $25 donation noise is a loud scream and a creepy doll gif pops up on stream. This sound alone has made me thousands of dollars because my viewers want to scare me while I'm playing, so they donate $25 to get the reaction from me and the reaction from other viewers in the chat.

I've done the same thing with a John Cena noise and gif popup. When people donate $50, a very loud John Cena noise plays and that has also created endless funny moments on stream. I've even named my Sunday streams Cena Sellout Sunday where we make the $50 Cena noise a big part of the stream. I know this may sound dumb or silly to you, but to my community, it's an inside joke and meme we understand. It's up to you to create those stream memes and jokes for your donation popups so you can earn more and have a tighter knit community. You don't need to have a bunch of unique popups to start, but over time, some stream defining moments will happen, and that may give you an idea for a funny popup. In time, you will find out what your stream loves, and it's up to you to package that love into something you can add to the donor's experience.

Text to Speech:

Another great way to give more value to your donors, and in turn get more donations, is to have text-to-speech enabled so that the person donating can leave you a message that gets read out loud on stream. This allows your viewers to be more of a part of the show. Most streamers have text-to-speech enabled using Streamlabs, and it's a very effective tool to earn more money during your stream.

Media Sharing:

Media sharing—also available through Streamlabs—allows the person who is donating to leave a YouTube clip that will play when they send in their donation. Think of this as a video or song request the donator can send for the entire stream to watch or listen to (be careful that the video they're sending isn't against Twitch's terms of service). Some streamers opt to only have media share open one day a week, while others like myself have it open all of the time. If you have media sharing enabled on your stream, you can very easily moderate what plays automatically and what has to be approved so that nothing offensive plays accidentally. If you don't already have media share enabled for your donations, then I suggest trying it out one day a week and see how it goes for your stream. If you don't like distractions while you're streaming, and you hate having to monitor each media share donation that comes through, then media share may not be a good fit for your stream.

Daily Donation Goal:

A daily donation goal is the closest way of asking for donations without ever verbally asking for them. Your daily donation goal could be $30, $50, or even $100 a day like mine. Some streamers don't use this tool because they don't want viewers to know how much they're making a day. There are normally two main reasons for this. The first is that they simply want to keep their income private and don't wish to share it with the world. The second is that some streamers think if the viewer knows they're making lots of money a day, then the viewers would be less likely to give more money. This, in my opinion, is horse shit. There are many streamers that show they have 50,000 paid subscribers and top donations in the thousands of dollars, yet they still get an endless amount of support from their communities. There are streamers making millions of dollars a year and people will still gladly give them donations big and small. Having a daily donation goal simply allows your viewers to see how you're doing for the day in donations.

Often times, if you've been streaming all day long with little to no donations, some of your viewers may step up and fill up that bar for you. A daily donation goal isn't for everyone, but if you haven't tried it out yet this might be a tool you could experiment with. The daily donation goal is great for smaller or medium-sized channels where donations can be a hit or a miss depending on the day. Once again Streamlabs is a great program to use to set up your daily donation goal.

The Big No-Nos:

Now that I've gone through the importance of how to handle all donations big and small, let me go through the things you should NEVER do to get donations.

Asking:

Even though you might have popups, a daily donation goal, and other tactics to help entice viewers to donate, it doesn't mean you should ever flat out ask for donations or guilt trip your viewers to give. It doesn't matter if your car broke down, you got laid off at work, or you just haven't been making great money lately. You're not a charity, so begging for money isn't the way to go. If you want to earn more money, find ways to give more value to your viewers and they will pay for it. Remember: Your viewers want to give you money, you just need to give them a reason, and the reason should never be a sob story. If you have a daily donation goal up on your stream, your viewers know what you would like to make in the run of a day. So put a smile on their faces and kick some ass in gaming and they will fill that donation bar for you.

What if you need money to go to an event like Pax East and it's too expensive for you to travel to out of pocket? Instead of a daily donation goal, perhaps you can put up a Pax East fund goal for a month before the event. This lets people know that the money they're donating is going to help get you to an event, so they can meet you and possibly help you get new sponsors while you're there. Once you put up that goal on the stream, you better be prepared to go to that event whether you get full funding from your stream or not. It wouldn't be fair if you only raised 25% of the trip and decided not to go. Ultimately you're never asking for money to go—you're letting people know that donations for the next month will go towards your trip to Pax East.

Once you're an established streamer getting donations becomes a normal occurrence, but you should never take it for granted. People are giving you their hard-earned money so you can continue to entertain them on a regular basis. Just be consistent with your streams and brighten peoples' days, and the money will come. If you're at the point where you're begging for money from your viewers so that you can continue to stream on a full-time basis, then you're already in over your head and need to reevaluate your business plan.

Overall, receiving donations can be an awkward thing. Someone you never met just gave you money or even paid your rent. If you grow up like me, where nothing was ever just handed to you, then it's a weird feeling. Just know that you're very blessed to have strangers around the world that care for you and support you. Be yourself and thank them from your heart. Let them know that it's not just the money they're giving, but it's the opportunity of being a full-time gamer that is the real gift. You as the streamer give them a positive escape from work or school and sometimes even help them through dark periods in their lives. In the end, both sides—the streamer and viewer—have each other's backs, and that's what creates a strong community.

Twitch Subscribers:

As both an Affiliate and Official Twitch Partner, you have the ability to make money from subscribers. There are currently three levels of paid subscribers: $4.99, $9.99, $24.99 a month. If you're an affiliate streamer, you will get a 50/50 split with Twitch. That means that for each $4.99 subscriber you will get ~$2.50. It's the same starting rate for a partner, but as you start to get more subscribers, Twitch can give you better rates. Partners aren't allowed to talk about their rates, but I can tell you I'm getting a much better rate than a 50/50 split. I personally don't know what qualifies you for a raise, but I had hundreds and hundreds of subscribers before I got a raise. The more money you're bringing into Twitch, the better rates you will likely get.

Good news though, as streamers are starting to see a bigger spike in their subscriber count because of Twitch Prime. Twitch Prime is a perk every Amazon Prime member gets. This perk is a free $4.99

paid subscription to a stream of their choosing every month. The streamer still gets the same rate as a normally paid subscription. I'll be straight up with you: at the time of writing this chapter I'm at 1,400 subscribers. This is a great base paycheck I know I'm going to get each month as long as I can keep my subscriptions around this number. This is great but it's nothing compared to streamers with 30,000, 40,000 or even 100,000 paid subscribers. There are streamers pulling in hundreds of thousands of dollars each and every month in subscriber money alone!

Tips for Getting More Subscribers:

Subscriber Daily Goal:

Just like a daily donation goal, a daily subscriber goal will allow your stream to see how many new subscriptions you received for the day. I personally had a five-subscriber-a-day goal for about six years, and just about every day I would crush that goal. Just last week I changed it from five per day to twenty per day, and the outcome has been amazing. I'm currently getting between twenty-five and forty new subscribers every day since I made that switch. It's incredible what a daily goal can do for your stream both with subscribers and donations. I mean, goals are meant to be reached right?

Subscriber Popups:

Much like donation popups, you can choose unique sounds and gifs to pop up when you get a new subscriber. For the longest time, one of my subscriber sounds was, "This new subscriber has a colossal, enormous, extensive, gigantic, giant, great, humongous, immense, magnificent, mammal-sized, massive cock!" This would make the stream laugh every time and people would subscribe because they wanted to be told they have such a huge penis. Of course I would remove this sound if I was doing any type of sponsored content, but on my regular streams this was one of many funny sounds that played for new subscribers. Think about what kind of sounds you can use to help your daily subscriber numbers grow.

Subscriber Trains:

Subscriber trains are a very effective tool that many successful streamers use. A subscriber train allows the viewers to work together to get a huge subscriber count before a timer runs out. Every time a new person subscribes, the timer gets reset back to the top. If someone doesn't subscribe before the timer ends, the train stops and a new train begins resetting the number of subscribers back to zero. Subscriber trains aren't very popular with small or medium sized streams. Normally, streamers with 10,000+ viewers use them.

Performing for Subscribers:

When hitting my subscriber goals for the day, I normally sing a song for my community. This creates a bit of hype to have my goal reached. You don't have to sing, but let's say you're a League of Legends player that only plays Leona or Graves. You can tell your stream that if you hit the daily goal you will reward them with playing a champion that the stream votes for. This gives more value to the viewer and that might be the thing that sells them on becoming a subscriber.

Subscriber Dedicated Games:

Many streamers have "Subscriber Sundays" where the streamer might play games with paid subscribers or the streamer might play a game voted for by subscribers. I've even seen streamers that restrict non-subscribers from chatting on stream for a day, but I don't suggest doing so unless you're a huge streamer with tens of thousands of viewers. The only reason why you would have a subscriber-only chat is to weed out the spam or block trolls from spoiling a game. If you're going to have a dedicated day for your subscribers, you should keep it to just one day a week. You don't want to alienate your non-subscribers as they might not be able to afford a subscription. Using subscriber dedicated games is a very effective way to increase demand for your potential subscribers, and you can even do it at the end of your streams for an hour or so.

Remind People About Twitch Prime:

A few times throughout your stream you can remind people that, if they're an Amazon Prime member, they do have access to a free Twitch Prime subscription. Many viewers forget to re-subscribe to a stream because sadly Twitch Prime subs aren't automatically renewed. Each month the viewer has to remember to subscribe again manually, so giving a friendly reminder to your stream about a free Twitch Prime sub can earn you a lot of new subscribers and re-subscriptions. Unlike donations, asking people to consider to subscribe if they're enjoying the content isn't rude and normally doesn't come off as begging.

I normally say something like this, " If you guys are enjoying the stream don't forget to finger bang that follow button, and if you want to take it a step further you can become a paid subscriber for that low price of $4.99 or a Twitch Prime sub." I say this in a joking manner, but it's serious enough that the community doesn't disregard what I'm saying, and normally I'll see a few new Twitch Prime or paid subscribers come through. I do this once every two hours or so. It's funny watching a streamer like Ninja plug Twitch Prime subscribers to his chat because the moment he does he gets dozens of subscribers every second.

The very <u>BEST</u> time to do your little subscriber plug is after something exciting happens on stream. Maybe that's a crazy game or an incredible play in Fortnite. Do your plug when your viewers are smiling, and they're far more likely to pull the trigger on becoming a subscriber. Don't do your sales pitch when nothing worth subscribing for is happening. Sure, you still may get a sub or two, but you're going to have a much bigger impact when excitement levels are high.

Merchandise:

Now that you have a greater understanding of the big three money makers—sponsorships, advertisements, and subscribers—let's talk about a couple of the smaller side hustles that will put a few more dollars in your pocket and help with your branding.

Selling merch isn't something I normally do, so to be honest, this isn't a subject I'm as experienced in as the rest of the streaming business. The last time I sold t-shirts and sweaters was back in 2012. I sold about 250 shirts and only made about $5 per shirt. For me, offering merch wasn't about making money, it was more about having my dedicated followers wearing my brand. Also, when your viewer owns a physical product of yours that they see on a regular basis, it's a constant reminder to them that you exist. One of the harder parts of being a streamer is staying relevant, and not having your viewers forget you and move on to someone else that is more consistent or active than you are.

If you're brand new to streaming, then I wouldn't worry about merch just yet. You should focus first on figuring out your brand and who you are as a streamer. Once you have a dedicated following and you know who you are as an entertainer, then look into creating merch. This could be t-shirts, sweaters, mouse pads, coffee mugs, stickers or whatever else you can slap your logo on. You can set up a merch store right through Streamlabs or you can use a 3rd party e-commerce site.

Amazon Affiliate Links:

Amazon Affiliate links are something streamers should consider setting up. You simply go to the affiliate area of Amazon's website and sign up. Once you're signed up, you can put your Amazon affiliate links at the bottom of your stream page and let people know that if they're going to buy things on Amazon to consider using your affiliate links before shopping. When they click on your affiliate link and shop, you will get a commission on everything they buy. I normally make $150–$200 a month off of my links and I never really mention them. I make considerably more around Christmas time when everyone is shopping for gifts, and I make sure to mention my links during the holiday season. This is a great way for your community to support you by spending money they were going to spend anyway.

The only downside to Amazon affiliate links is it takes a while to set up. It can be time consuming to create the links, but in the end it's worth it if you have a decent-sized following. If you're a new streamer, this isn't something you should be focused on. Once you're an established streamer, then adding these side hustles is great.

Hopefully this chapter helped you gain a deeper understanding of how to earn more money with your stream. If you work to understand the psychology of the viewer and give them more of what they want, they'll reward you. Add more value, and you'll earn more money. The more money you earn, the longer you can continue this great career. All of my tips and tricks aren't for everyone, but I'm sure if you gave a few of them a try you'd be blown away with the results. Tweet at me @LAGTVMB and let me know what the biggest thing you've learned from this chapter is. Also, if you want some one-on-one coaching from me, head over to The Grind website and I'd love to help you grow your business.

Quick Notes:

1. Remember: It's OK to make as much money as you can with your stream.

2. Know your monetary worth as a streamer. This will help you get the best deals with sponsors.

3. Consider working with an agent, exclusive or non-exclusive.

4. Reach out and contact sponsors yourself if you don't have an exclusive deal with an agent.

5. Run ads on your stream at the right times.

6. Customize Streamlabs alerts for subscriptions and donations.

7. STOP settling and earn more money with your stream!

CHAPTER 6

TRANSITIONS

As a streamer, you're going to go through many transitions, and some of them will take you to new heights, while others will have you playing catch up. Maybe you're planning to quit your day job and stream full-time, or perhaps you're being forced to change your main game because it's no longer popular. Transitions or changes in any area of your life can be a very scary thing. As humans, we are creatures of habit, so changing our routine—in big or small ways—can cause anxiety and self-doubt. It's important that you fully understand the position you're currently in and weigh the pros and cons of a change you're about to make.

In this chapter, I'm going to share with you the steps I took before becoming a full-time gamer, along with some of the streaming transitions I've made that have helped me grow to new heights.

When Should You Become a Full-Time Streamer?

The answer to this question is different for everyone, but every streamer should have a full understanding of their current financial and living situation before quitting their day job. If you have kids or other dependents, you'll really have to make sure that if you quit your day job, you can still provide for your loved ones. If you're riding solo fresh out of school, you may be willing to take on a bit more risk to follow your dreams. I'm not saying if you have kids and/or a significant other that you can't stream full-time—there are many part-time and full-time streamers that have a family and are doing well. I'm just saying if you have those things, I wouldn't suggest quitting your day job the moment you think you're making enough money gaming—it requires more thought and calculation.

For instance, you probably want to save up a reasonable emergency fund just in case you have down periods in streaming income after you quit your job.

When I first started making YouTube videos and streaming, I never once thought about quitting my day job and going full time with gaming. It wasn't until I started making a little over a thousand dollars a month when I started to fantasize about walking into work and giving my two weeks' notice. So, I set out a goal to pay off all of my debts and save up $5,000 in case streaming didn't work out after I quit my day job. I started to grind even more hours into streaming and saved up just about every dollar I was making outside of the bills I had to pay. It got to the point where I was making more money streaming then I was at my day job, but I still kept my day job for a few months to have that second income and increase my emergency fund.

On September 18th, 2011, with $5,000 in the bank, I drove into work and gave my boss my two weeks' notice.

Funnily enough, it was a very slow day in the restaurant and I got cut from my shift. I ordered some food and went to the kitchen to see if it was ready and by that time all of the kitchen staff heard I was going to be quitting. There were a few cooks that liked to smoke weed, and I hadn't touched weed since high school. From time to time after work, the boys would ask me if I wanted to smoke with them and I always said no. A couple of years earlier one of the kitchen guys asked me, "What is it going to take to get you to smoke a joint with me?" I foolishly said, "The last day I work here I'll smoke a joint with you guys." As I'm waiting for my food, one of the chefs says, "So in two weeks you gonna smoke up with us?" I laughed, "Sure, in two weeks, I'll get high with you." Just as I said that my boss came into the kitchen and said, "The new girl is willing to take your shifts for the next two weeks, so if you want to be a free man now, you can." I instantly said yes, and just like that I no longer had a day job. The cook said with a huge smile, "I'm off in fifteen and the joints are already rolled." I started laughing my ass off, grabbed my food and had lunch. Once the kitchen guys were done their shift, I smoked weed for the first time in at least six years. I got so high I ordered more food and sat at my old work for hours before heading home.

Even though I went in excited to give my two weeks' notice, having my money saved in the bank let me skip the two weeks with confidence that things would work out. I personally think everyone planning to leave their day job should have a reserve fund of cash for worst case scenarios and it will alleviate some of the financial pressures while making such a huge transition.

If you have a significant other in your life, allow them to voice their concerns about the transition and work together to formulate a plan so you can make your dreams a reality. It's normal for your spouse or family to have some doubt. I mean, you're talking about quitting your job to play video games. Work hard and prove to them this is for real and you're going to make it work. As you become more successful and happier in your own life, it will rub off on the ones around you. Just know that when you quit your day job and go full-time, you're going to need to bust your ass harder than ever before. The hours you were working at your old job now need to become more streaming hours and time spent building your community. Many streamers get complacent and become lazy because the freedom of no day job can often be a gateway to procrastination. When you have a day job your boss expects you to show up on time every day or you will be fired. Now you're the boss, and there's no one around to hold you accountable. So, you need to stay disciplined and never lose focus for too long or you're going to end up working for "the man" again.

Transitioning from One Game to Another:

One of the scariest things for a streamer to do is switch their main game. The moment you even entertain the idea of switching your focus to another game, people in your community might be upset because you're known for playing a certain game.

The bigger a streamer you are, the easier a switch can be. This is why the mega streamers can jump on any popular game as they have a massive core fan base that will watch them play anything. It doesn't matter what they play—they will be the top-viewed streamer for that game. As a smaller streamer, it's a massive risk and one that could cut your livelihood in half or more. If you're not a variety streamer, the only time you should be looking to switch main games is if your main game is dying, or if you're seriously unhappy playing your current game. If you're seriously unhappy, just like a job, you can't simply quit right away without consequences. People normally don't quit their day job until they have something else lined up, it's the same thing with streaming.

You will lose tons of viewers, and it will be an uphill battle, but if you do it smartly, you can do it well. The key to making a switch is to figure out what your current viewership is with your core fan base and why they like you so much. Your core fan base is made up of diehard fans who love you as a person and would watch you playing any game.

I've personally gone from Starcraft 2 to World Of Warcraft, to League of Legends, back to Starcraft 2, to Paragon, to Runescape, to Realm Royale, and back to Starcraft 2 where I am currently. I've had major success in switching games. I've also had some major failures that I'll walk you through. In general, understood that my core fan base loved when I sang songs, put on chainmail, and did crazy shit. I just took that formula and repeated it in other communities.

I knew Starcraft 2 was dropping off in popularity. While Twitch as a whole was growing rapidly, those new eyes weren't coming for Starcraft, they were coming for League of Legends at the time. I had to formulate a plan to break into the LoL community. Here's how I did it: First I played Starcraft 2 for 4–6 hours. This would keep my viewers happy, and it would allow me to achieve my peak concurrent viewership. Then, when I was at my peak, I would switch over to League of Legends with already over 1,000 viewers. This would put me in the top two rows in the Twitch directory for League of Legends and I would start to have a bunch of new viewers check out my stream. Sure, I would lose a bunch of Starcraft viewers, but I still had a big enough core fan base to keep me near the top. Over time, new viewers started pouring in and I was reaching new viewership highs in League of Legends. They would pop in and see me singing songs, and I would hook them as viewers.

I was pretty trash at League of Legends when I started out, so I just had to be funny and make fun of myself and it worked. Every day after Starcraft 2 I would play League of Legends, and within a couple weeks I was getting over 3,000 concurrent viewers in

League of Legends while making more money than I had been while playing Starcraft.

Testing the waters with a new game is scary, but if you transition slowly so that you don't shock your viewership, you have the best chance for success. You have to show your viewers you're just as entertaining playing the new game as you were playing the old one. It's risky, but there can be massive benefits in terms of viewership and your own personal happiness if you pull it off.

Sometimes, making the switch doesn't work out. Recently I fell in love with a game called Realm Royale. This was an up-and-coming Battle Royale game that had a lot of promise. I decided I was going to play this game full-time in the hopes that it would blow up in popularity and I'd be there to reap the benefits. I dedicated more than six weeks of my time getting very good at the game. In the meantime, I had to deal with having all-time low viewership numbers and a huge drop in paid subscriber count. I didn't mind taking the hit in money because I could afford it and my core fan base was still supporting me. Unfortunately, Realm Royale kept making bad decisions, and it ultimately killed their game.

There I was with 600 paid subscribers, an all-time low for me in six years, but the worst part was I was mentally defeated. I knew how much work it was going to take to get my viewership back up and the subscriber counts back past 1,000. This was demoralizing and I was nearly ready to accept the fact that I had an amazing career and maybe this was going to be my new norm.

I was tired of grinding and not in the burnt-out way. For the first time in my career, I was only putting in 30 hours a week streaming. I was starting to see how this affected not only my earnings but also my attitude towards streaming.

Just days later my wife told me she was pregnant and that changed my outlook once again. There I was, ready to just coast on the rest of my streaming career and reject any thoughts of grinding again. I quickly got out of the pity party I was throwing and started grinding Starcraft 2 again. After just a month of streaming between eight and ten hours a day—and changing my mentality to get hungry again—

my viewership more than doubled again, and my subscribers rose to 1,400.

The reason why I'm telling you this is because as a streamer you're going to face down periods and have self-doubt. Don't let those feelings deter you from what you're good at. Pick yourself up and if you have to go back to your default game and grind, do it. Not every transition will go as smoothly as it did for me with League of Legends. Just make sure you're mentally prepared for the drop-in viewers up front and if you're going to make a switch, then give it all you've got. Don't half-ass it—you need to bring the same level of passion to the new game as you did the old.

Quick Notes:

1. Have a full understanding of your financial situation before ever quitting your day job to stream full-time.

2. Make sure you're making a consistent paycheck for three to six months before entertaining the idea of going full-time as a streamer.

3. Have an emergency fund of money saved up as a "buffer" in case your stream has a down period.

4. Have a full understanding of the pros and cons of switching your main game. Try playing your main game for a few hours to get normal peak viewership before switching into another game you're interested in pursuing.

5. Don't beat yourself up over a drop-in viewership when making a main game transition. Stay focused and bring the same level of energy to the new game as you did the old and hopefully the transition will be one with great success.

CHAPTER 7

NETWORKING & GROWING YOUR STREAM

Are you tired of streaming with next to no viewers and little to no chat activity? Well, in this chapter I'm going to share ten tips to help you grow your viewership and improve your network.

1) Collaborating with Other Streamers:

Collaborating with other streamers can help your stream numbers grow exponentially. Collaborating allows both streamers to have access to their respective communities. If you have good chemistry with the streamer and viewers are having a good time, the viewers are more likely to watch you when their favorite streamer isn't online. You can collaborate no matter what level streamer you are. For example, you might be a Fortnite streamer with twenty viewers. If you get to know another Fortnite streamer with around the same viewership numbers, you two could possibly duo queue with each other. If that other streamer has twenty viewers, now you're playing in front of 40 viewers. Even if you make an impact on five of his or her viewers, your concurrent viewership numbers could go up 25% or more. This is a very powerful networking strategy that can help both parties.

2) Being Active in Other Streamers' Chats:

I spoke about this earlier in the book, but I'll mention it again. If you want to have a community around you, you need to be part of the community. For example, if you stream PlayerUnknown's Battlegrounds (PUBG), you should go to other PUBG streamers on your free time and be active in their chat. Make positive comments about their gameplay and ask questions. When the appropriate time presents itself, let the streamer know you also stream the game. You must make sure to NEVER self-promote out of the blue. You might be there to do some networking, but you want your networking to be natural. If that natural opportunity to share a bit about yourself doesn't happen, then move on. It's rude to go to someone's stream to just promote your own. It's a great way to get banned and burn a bridge.

It's important to hang out on a stream that you enjoy, and don't just stick around because you think you can leach their viewers. That's not the mission—the mission is to create genuine connections with other communities. These connections may take days or months to build and sometimes the streamer on the other end has no interest in working with you. That's ok, move on and keep introducing yourself to communities and be active in their chat. Just remember to be respectful.

3) Hosting:

Hosting and getting hosted can have a profound impact on a stream. Hosting is a feature Twitch implemented where a streamer can send his or her entire viewership over to another streamer. This often happens when the hostee ends his or her stream for the day. Having dozens, hundreds or even thousands of viewers raid your stream can be life-changing. So much so that many new streamers believe that if they just got a host from a big streamer, they would make it as a full-time streamer.

Getting hosted is great if you're ready for it. First impressions are everything if you're a new streamer, and if you're not entertaining, getting hosted for 1,000 viewers would likely be a waste. Those 1,000 viewers would show up and leave. When I get hosted for a large number of viewers, I go into show mode and start singing. This hooks a lot of new viewers immediately and they get a taste of what my stream is all about right away. At that point they will hit the follow button or leave right away. It's a love or hate thing. When you get hosted, you need to thank the person that's hosting and introduce yourself to the new viewers. Start talking with them and get them engaged with you and your community. This builds a connection with the new viewers before most of them leave.

You could get hosted by the biggest streamer in the world and have fifteen minutes of fame, but it's what you do with that fifteen minutes that's important. Hosting can be a powerful tool when used right. I suggest at the end of your streams, try to host a streamer with around the same viewership as you to increase the odds they will host you back. If you keep hosting the same streamer over and over and he or she doesn't ever return the favor, then stop hosting them and host someone else. The other streamer just might return the favor one day. Spread the love, and love will come back to you.

4) Social Media Postings:

I believe streamers should post on social media every time they go live. This allows your followers to see via Twitter, Facebook, and even Instagram that there is a new stream up. During your streams, you should always mention to your viewers to follow you on social media. Have your social network links at the bottom of your stream, or have a chatbot post them in your Twitch chat every 30 minutes. About 20% of my viewership comes from social media postings. You can see and track these analytics on your Twitch dashboard.

5) YouTube:

YouTube has been a very powerful tool for me personally. Our YouTube series "When Cheese Fails" became the biggest Starcraft 2 series on YouTube, so I started plugging my stream in my YouTube videos. This helped grow my Justin.TV & Twitch streams early on and things snowballed from there.

If you don't already have a YouTube channel, create one. You can use this YouTube channel as a VOD from your twitch streams, featuring funny clips or high-level gameplay. It's as simple as highlighting your Twitch past broadcasts and uploading those clips to YouTube. This will allow people on YouTube to discover your videos and from there they will see that you stream on Twitch. A lot of very popular Twitch streamers got their big break from posting videos on YouTube and converting those viewers to Twitch. Not to mention if your YouTube channel starts to generate a lot of views, you'll earn a nice pay check each month from YouTube, and it's another place to advertise potential sponsors.

Growing on YouTube can be even harder than growing on Twitch, so don't get discouraged if your YouTube videos aren't getting a lot of views. It only takes one random video to go viral for you to suddenly be seen by thousands or even millions of people. Keep grinding out those quality clips from your stream to YouTube, and in time you'll start to see progress in your views.

6) Dedicated Stream Helper:

Having a dedicated viewer to help you with highlighting great stream clips and posting funny moments on forums for you can be a massive help. Almost every big Twitch streamer has hired someone to do this kind of work for them so they can stay focused on streaming long hours. Even as a small streamer, getting a close friend or dedicated viewer to post the odd funny or epic stream moment on Reddit can help you grow exponentially. It's normally frowned upon for you to post your own clips on Reddit, but if a fan does it then it's fair game. Just don't abuse this tactic—a fantastic post once or twice a month is more than enough. If you're doing it all the time, readers on Reddit will get tired of seeing your face. I've had fans post funny clips of me on Reddit that helped my channel grow immensely. Make sure you're putting out quality because as discussed before first impressions are <u>EVERYTHING</u>!

7) Giveaways:

Doing giveaways once in a while can help get your stream in front of new viewers. If you put giveaway in your Twitch title, this will attract people looking for free stuff. The biggest problem with using this tactic is once the giveaway is gone so are the viewers. So, when you do the giveaway, make sure to ask them to follow you on social media and your Twitch stream for a chance to win.

You don't need to spend tons of money on your giveaway. Giving away $50 in Fortnite V-bucks will have the same effect as giving away $500 worth of V-bucks. Think of it as an investment and ask your accountant if you can claim that as advertising dollars for your business. Just make sure that if you're doing giveaways, you have the talent or entertainment value to hold potential new viewers after the giveaway is done. There's no point in spending a bunch of money for viewers if you don't know how to hold their attention outside of a giveaway.

8) Streaming Marathons:

One of the classic ways to gain new viewers is to do 24-hour streams. There's something about watching someone torture themselves playing video games for a whole day that people love. I used to do these when I started out and they were really helpful. Make sure that you're playing a game that is fairly popular—there's no point in doing a 24-hour live stream playing something like Mirror's Edge unless you're a speed runner and that's all you do. You need to play a game where there's a ton of viewer traffic. Make sure to put 24-hour marathon in your stream title and have a timer on stream so new viewers can see how far in you are. It's important to drink lots of water and get up and move around every hour or so. Gaming for 24 hours straight isn't the healthiest thing to do, so don't go overboard and try and stream for 48 or 72 hours. People have died from extreme exhaustion. Listen to your body. If you've streamed for fifty hours and you're overly tired, then get offline and get some rest. Your health is important, and if you get sick or your sleep schedule is messed up for the next week, then the 24-hour marathon may actually be counterproductive.

9) Attending Live Events:

Attending live events like TwitchCon or Pax East is a great place to network. You'll be able to meet and chat with other streamers and meet viewers that watch your stream. Attending panels at these events can also be a great source of information to help you in your career. The biggest reason why I go is to meet new potential sponsors. There are dozens of companies at these events looking to give out sponsorship deals. Hand out business cards, shake some hands, and use lots of hand sanitizer!

10) Streaming Schedule:

Having a streaming schedule and being consistent with it is a great way to grow your stream. It's important that if you have a streaming schedule that you stick to it. If you become unreliable with your schedule, your viewership will take a hit. If you can't commit to the same schedule every week that's ok. Some streamers give a schedule a week in advance, so viewers know when they can expect you each week. You can let viewers know right in your Twitch via a chatbot, or you could post and pin your schedule on Twitter. Consistency is the most important thing as a streamer. If you don't want to have a streaming schedule that's fine, just try to have some kind of pattern to your streaming hours so when you do stream, your viewers have an idea about when you're likely going to be live.

Quick Notes:

1. Network and collaborate with other streamers your size.

2. Use social media to let everyone know you're going live. Twitter, Facebook, and Instagram are commonly used by streamers.

3. Spread the love - host and raid other streamers your size. The good karma will come back to you time.

4. Consider creating a YouTube channel as a VOD for your streams.

5. Have a trusted moderator or community member help you with highlights and posting your content on YouTube or forums.

CHAPTER 8

PROS & CONS OF STREAMING

As a streamer who's been through it all, there are tons of pros and cons to this job. Some of you may already relate to some of these topics, while others may learn some valuable information about how to grow your business, and what to expect along the way.

Pro #1: Playing Video Games for a Living:

I think most of us can agree that playing video games for a living is incredible. I've been a gamer since I got the Super Nintendo back in 1991. Video games have always been a healthy escape for me, and the fact I can do this for a living is amazing and I'm grateful for the opportunity.

Con #1: Playing Video Games for a Living:

Yes, playing video games for a living can be a con to some. In the past 7 years, I have put in maybe twenty hours of personal (i.e., not streaming) gaming. It's extremely hard for a lot of streamers to want to play games for fun outside of work. You are turning a fun pastime into your day job. Most streamers that have been doing this for years no longer use video games as an escape. I'm not saying you can't have fun playing video games anymore on your own, but it will feel weird and chances are you'll rather be doing something else.

Pro #2: Video Games & Equipment Become Write-Offs:

Before I get started, I want to make it clear: I'm not an accountant or a tax professional. This is not tax advice. Take what I say and ask a professional about it. I highly suggest getting an accountant to help you with your bookkeeping.

In order for my business to generate money I need to have several things like a computer, audio equipment, video games, internet, office space and I may even have to travel to events for networking purposes. One of the great benefits I take advantage of every year are the tax write-offs. Anything I buy for my business is a business expense, and at the end of the year I can get a kickback on the things I bought. These benefits may differ from country to country so make sure you speak to a tax professional to see which items you can claim on your taxes. This may allow you to spend a bit more money on better gear to improve your stream and gain more viewers. Keep all of your receipts. It doesn't matter if you commission some artwork for your brand or pay your cell phone bill so you can stay up to date on your social media accounts. You're running a business, so treat it like one, and you'll be surprised by the amount of money you will save each year on things you had no idea you could claim. If you're not already taking advantage of the things I've listed, and you're allowed to by law where you're from, then you're cheating yourself out of potentially thousands of dollars a year. GET AN ACCOUNTANT!

Con #2: Taxes

As a streamer, it's your responsibility to keep track of the money you earn, and have a chunk of it ready to be paid to the government at the end of the year. A lot of streamers don't understand this, and they spend all of their money. Next thing they know they're neck deep in debt because they didn't prepare their books correctly. Having to keep track of all of this is a pain in the ass, and it isn't fun for anyone. There's more to streaming than just playing games. This other side to business—bookkeeping—is overlooked by many entrepreneurs. I know I've said this multiple times now, but you must speak to professionals to help you run your business. I don't care if you're making $10,000 a year or a million dollars a year. Hire someone to help you, and guess what? You can likely claim your accountant bill as a write-off. When your books are taken care of, you will be able to focus 100% of your energy on streaming and making money. If not, the burden of bookkeeping will rent space in your head, and this entire process won't be fun to go through.

Pro #3: The Dirty Esports Money

I'm sure you've seen the amount of money some streamers make. Hell, I've done very well from streaming, and I'm not even close to the level others are at. Earning a great living doing what you love is, in my opinion, the definition of success. Being able to provide for your family and being a self-made man or woman is an incredible accomplishment. Most people aren't going to make a million dollars a year—most streamers won't even make six figures a year—but if you're happy and you can provide for your family from streaming and it's what you love, there is no better feeling.

Con #3: Oversaturation

Twitch has grown from a small side project to a multi-billion-dollar company. With that came a massive wave of new streamers wanting a piece of the pie. When I started, I was first to market. So naturally, I grew with the company. Now when you get started as a streamer, it can be very intimidating because there is so much competition. These days it's more about finding your niche and growing from there. It's not as easy now as it was to become a Twitch star back in 2012–2013. Now everyone and their dog wants to be the next Ninja. Rightfully so, it's an exciting job and anyone can apply for it. Just know, even considering all of the competition, it's not impossible to make a living these days on Twitch or any other streaming service, it just requires more effort and a bit more patience.

Pro #4: Working from Home

Have you ever dreamed about working from home? Ever dream about not having to wake up extra early to beat traffic and pay for public transportation or gas money? Well, as a streamer, one of the biggest pros to the job is working from home. It's important that, if you can, set up your office away from everyone else in the house. It's important that you stay focused on your work while you're working. It's easy to be distracted or procrastinate when you're already home. When you stay disciplined with your streaming hours while working from home, it's going to be hard to ever want to work away from home again.

Con #4: Working from Home

Working from home can be mentally draining. You must have time throughout the week to leave your house. It's so easy to get obsessed with streaming when you're 30 feet away from your computer 24 hours a day. Going out for a walk, a drive, or seeing a movie is something I do on a regular basis. Even me writing this book is done at local coffee shops so that I have some time away from home. Spending too much time at home can be extremely isolating and lonely. Just walking around near other people does so much for me mentally. I can easily lock myself in the basement and stream 80 hours a week if I don't force myself to get out and get some fresh air. You should always find a hobby outside of your home and away from the streaming PC, even if it is only a few times a week.

Pro #5: Gaining New Friends in Your Community

It doesn't matter if you have three viewers or 30,000 viewers, you will become friends with people that are tuning into your stream on a regular basis. I have become personal friends with many community members over the years, and those friendships will last a lifetime. Going to live events like Pax East, I've gotten to meet and spend time with dozens of viewers that are now personal friends of mine. Before streaming, I normally wouldn't go out of my way to try and meet new people, but streaming gave me the opportunity to meet people with the same interests as me. You even see streamers getting married to other streamers they've met online. If you're looking for some new friends, streaming will present you tons of opportunities to meet new people.

Con #5: Lack of Privacy

One of the biggest deal breakers for new streamers getting into the business is their lack of privacy. The more personal you get with your community, the more information they will have about you. It's a good feeling when someone sees you out in public and says they enjoy watching your stream, but it's not a good feeling when people show up at your door. The more famous you get the more steps you have to take to ensure your privacy and safety. It's not out of the norm for well-known streamers to move to gated communities. Some streamers become celebrities and are forced to take drastic measures to have some kind of privacy. Some streamers love the attention, while others hate it. I would suggest you keep very personal or private matters to your family and friends unless you're ok with everyone knowing.

Pro #6: Helping People in a Time of Need

Gaming communities do an insane amount of charity work each year and raise millions of dollars for great causes. But there's another type of giving that the public normally doesn't hear about, and that's helping a viewer through a tough time in their life. There could be a viewer or multiple viewers going through a very tough time in their lives and watching you puts a smile on their face. I've received many emails from viewers over the years thanking me for being a safe and healthy escape for them. There is no better feeling for me as a streamer than to know my stream helped someone in a time of need. So, the next time you feel like you're not having an impact on Twitch because you have a low view count, think twice.

Just because you don't hear about it, doesn't mean you're not making a difference.

Con #6: Dealing with Haters, Trolls, and Negativity

I could write an entire book on this subject alone. If you're a female streamer, you have no doubt been harassed by immature assholes. If you're a minority streamer, you will deal with racism. If you're overweight, you will be made fun of. Twitch chat and social media can be like high school all over again, and for a lot of us, high school was some of the worst years of our lives. The internet can be a hateful place and forming thick skin is a must if you want to stay sane in this industry.

I've personally been called every racist profanity you can think of. I've had people verbally attack my wife. I've had people wish death on myself and loved ones. Just two days ago someone wished death to my unborn baby. On a daily basis, people come to my stream to do nothing but spread hate or try to get a reaction. You must understand that the haters are a vocal minority, and you need to learn to simply ban and ignore them. Sometimes they will catch you on an "off day," when your guard is down, and you will feed the troll with a reaction. This is what they want—they are searching for attention because they aren't getting attention in real life.

No one deserves to be hated because of their ethnicity, weight, gender, or sexual orientation. Sadly, it happens a lot. It's good practice to have some trusted moderators in your chat to remove these assholes quickly. Whatever insecurities you have about yourself or your stream, dedicated trolls will feed on these and try to use them against you. Try and focus on the positive and don't let the haters win. The more successful you become, the more negativity you will face.

As a streamer, you're going to make mistakes. You're going to say things on stream that you'll later regret, you might even do something in your personal life that you're embarrassed or ashamed of. You need to forgive yourself and move forward. I've said things I regret on stream several years ago that people still remind me of today. When you're live streaming most hours of the day for years, you're bound to have moments of weakness and say or do some dumb shit. Sometimes the criticism you're getting is warranted and shouldn't be ignored. Sometimes you'll have to change your behavior a bit in order to have your chat change its behavior. If you're chill and relaxed, then your chat is likely going to be chill and relaxed. If you're a shock value streamer and you're very trolly, then your chat is probably going to be a spam-filled trolly chat. If you show up on stream in a bad mood and are being negative, your stream chat will follow suit.

Knowing the difference between legitimately constructive criticism and hate is key to managing your community. The best way to know if you personally should consider making a change in your behavior is if that vocal minority becomes the majority, or if in your heart you know what you're doing is wrong. Streaming video games and building a community is supposed to be fun—don't let a handful of attention seekers discourage you from following your dreams and enjoying the process.

CHAPTER 9

STREAMER HEALTH

Gaining traction with your stream causes a euphoric feeling. When your stream numbers are growing, you're having fun, possibly making more money than you ever have in your life, and fans are showering you with compliments—it's really a rush like no other. I became addicted to that rush, so much so that nothing else in my life really mattered. All I wanted to do was stream 10 hours a day, seven days a week, and keep growing. So that's what I did for the first five years. In doing so, my stream became very popular and I was able to change my life financially, but other parts of my life suffered.

I didn't have any real balance in my life. I rarely saw my friends, and on a good week, I got to spend three to five hours with my wife. She was working a full-time job, too, so when she was sleeping, I was working, and when I was working, she was sleeping. This was very tough at times on our relationship as communication was limited but she knew how much this opportunity meant to me and she never once gave me an ultimatum. Not every spouse will be this understanding and patient, so if you have a partner, you must learn to balance streaming and real life. Grinding your stream ten hours a day, seven days a week can be a good thing—in moderation. For example, say a new Call of Duty comes out and there's a huge opportunity to grow when it launches. If that's the case, then go ahead and bang out a 70–80-hour week. Just realize that you can't do that for months or years on end because you're going to get burnt out.

Being a streamer can be extremely isolating. You spend your entire day in your office that's normally in your house and then you walk to your bed and sleep. Unlike most 9–5 jobs where you leave your house and travel to your workplace and interact with other people, as streamer your interaction is with usernames in Twitch chat. If you don't have a significant other in your life, it can be even more isolating. I'm sure all of you have seen at least one streamer have a mental breakdown on stream or on Twitter about them feeling depressed or lost. I can tell you that streamer depression is real, and I've gone through it many times. I have personally seen psychologists to help me through tough spots in my career.

Having the pressure of being "on" all the time and dealing with criticism and hate negatively affected my personal wellbeing. Video games used to be my escape from all the bullshit going on in my life and now suddenly they were work. The last thing I ever want to do is play more video games after I'm done streaming.

My last big mental breakdown was two years ago. I was putting in extremely long hours and wasn't taking care of my health. I was gaining weight, and my immune system was shot. I ended up having an anxiety attack at about 2 am after a stream. I panic drove to the medical office my wife worked at, and a nurse there looked at me. My blood pressure was through the roof, and I thought I was dying. She rushed me to the hospital and the doctor said it was an anxiety attack.

All the pressure and stress, combined with not eating and sleeping properly, finally took its toll on me. From that point on I knew I needed to make a change, and I did. Instead of streaming ten hours a day six or seven days a week, I cut it down to 8–9 hours a day 5–6 days a week. I also forced myself to leave the house and exercise. Going to the gym allowed me to stay physically healthy while at the same time being around other people. I also go to the movies once a week just to leave the house and have a positive escape from everything.

I changed my work schedule a bit as well. I started streaming a bit earlier in the day so that I can end the stream between 10–11pm, allowing me to spend some quality time with my wife. Making these changes and cutting back on streaming hours did lower the amount of money I was making, but I became so much richer in life. I'm so much happier to have a life outside of streaming. You need to understand that if you have these mental breakdowns like I did, it's only going to affect your stream in a negative way. You're going to be moodier on stream, and when you do inevitably take time off to get your shit together temporarily, you're going to dread going back because all that time you took off means your viewer and subscriber count is going to be lower. That's when you'll realize you're going to have to put in even more hours to get back what you lost.

Assholes on your stream will passive-aggressively ask you things like "What happened to all your viewers?" Ignore them. When streamers fall, they fall hard, and they blame themselves because they're the ones running the show. Don't be so hard on yourself. Remember that playing video games for a living is fun. If you take care of your physical and mental health, you're going to have better streams. When you're in a good mood and having fun, so will your viewers.

It was really hard for me to admit that I was struggling. Most people in my life looked up to me like I had it all together. I was busy trying to help everyone around me and not myself. It's okay to open up to your family and friends. If they don't get how you're complaining about playing video games while they have to do "hard labor" then go talk to a professional like I did. You don't always have to be superman or superwomen, no matter how successful you are as a streamer. Your kryptonite will be the insane number of hours you have to put into your stream to really make it in this industry. You can still put in 60 hours a week if that's what you want, just find a balance for your health and relationships.

We as streamers think that if we take a day off, then our viewers will move on and forget about us. That just isn't true—your viewers will understand you taking time off for yourself. They are human as well and realize the importance of having a life outside of work. If you're on the grind and want to take a personal day, then do it! There's nothing wrong with that and you shouldn't feel guilty. For the first few years of my career, I used to hate taking a day off. I used to think that every day off was just me losing money and new followers. Yes, I would lose out on money for that day, but taking a day off would recharge my batteries for another week's grind. Ironically enough, if I didn't take a day off from time to time, then I would end up losing more money because I would get burnt out. Now, if you're a full-time streamer or working towards it, you shouldn't be taking three or four days off in a row a few times a month. Remember as a full-time streamer you still need to put in long hours, you just need to take a day or two off in between those long streaming stretches.

Stay the fuck away from drugs to help you stream. Taking drugs like Adderall to be more focused and play longer is the wrong way of doing it. These drugs can be addictive and cause a mountain of problems. If you're already streaming eight to ten hours a day six or seven days a week, then that's enough. You don't need to be pulling fifteen hours a day every day. It's not healthy, and you're going to crash hard. High-profile streamers have come out and admitted that drugs have negatively affected their health, and no good comes out of taking them.

It's also important for your mental health to keep some parts of your life private. Streamers that have a good personal connection with their communities often have the urge to share every part of their life publicly. Remember, whatever you share can be used against you in a negative way. If you're having a family crisis or a deeply personal issue, publicly talking about it might not be the best course of action. Calling a helpline or seeking professional help may be the right thing to do to start. When you're in a good head space, then you might consider sharing a positive message with your community on how you got out of the bad head space, which might help someone else going through a tough time.

I've just seen so many streamers pour their souls out publicly, only to deal with trolls that can make things worse. Once again, this is just a suggestion. If you want to share everything in your life, then go for it. I personally got married on Twitch in front of 50,000 people and it was a great thing to share with the world. There are intimate things about myself and family that I haven't shared publicly because, at the end of the day, it's not anyone's business. You should be able to feel like you have some kind of private life outside of your online persona. If you don't then streaming can take over every part of your being, and if your stream goes downhill, you will too. Find that balance.

97

Quick Notes:

1) **<u>GET OUT OF THE HOUSE!</u>** Yes, there's a world outside of your stream.

2) Stay in shape. It's important to get some exercise a few days a week. This will give you more energy for your streams and will improve your health overall.

3) If you're ever feeling down or depressed, talk to a loved one or seek professional help. There's a lot of pressure and criticism being in the public's eye, so reach out if you feel it's too much to handle at any given moment.

4) Don't share everything about yourself with the world. Keep some things private. It's important for you to feel like you have some private and personal life outside of streaming.

5) Stay away from "performance-enhancing drugs," they will only create problems.

EPILOGUE: GOING FORWARD

Just eight years ago I was living in a bedbug-infested apartment in the ghetto. Today, I have a home, a beautiful wife, three pets, a baby boy on the way, and a very supportive online community. I'm extremely grateful for all of the support over the years. It's been a hell of a journey to get to this point. I've made mistakes along the way but learned a great deal about myself in the process. I put in the work, but you all were there to support it, and I thank you all for changing my life. I've even had the privilege to meet and become friends with some of my community members, and I'm sure those friendships will last a lifetime.

To people looking in from the outside, we might be just a community of nerds playing video games, but we are truly more than that. We've built an online family—a safe haven for people to escape from the hardships of life—even if it is just for an hour or two. You all have been my safe haven. I was in a very dark place when I started streaming. My friends around me were all starting careers and getting married, and there I was: a university dropout, in debt, homeless, with no motivation to change. I put out a couple of YouTube videos which some of you watched and it gave me purpose. I know it may sound pathetic, but that's honestly where I was. You all continued to support me while I figured out who I was, not only as an entertainer but also a person. Whether you're a fan of my content or not, I hope you got something out of this book. I never planned to write a book in my lifetime but here I am, and once again many of you are here to support it. I know I won't be able to stream forever and I'm okay with that. Everyone has a shelf life in this industry, but just know I'll be around for as long as you're willing to watch.

If you've made it this far into the book, you should now be equipped with the tools to get better results with your stream. I want to take this time to say thank you for purchasing this book and, if you enjoyed it, head over to Amazon and give it a review. If you're already a streamer and feel like the information in this book is worth knowing, then share it with your community and spread the word. For more streaming information and up-to-date content head over to www.TheGrind.gg

Now it's time for you to get on THE GRIND!

Stay Bouse,

MaximusBlack

ABOUT THE AUTHOR

Jeffrey Johnston, better known as "MaximusBlack" was one of Twitch's first partners back in 2011 and he is still streaming with great success today. He's also the co-creator of the hit YouTube series When Cheese Fails.

MaximusBlack has played on three professional Esports teams and clocked in over 14,000 hours of Twitch streaming. Now he's sharing his industry knowledge to help other streamers on The Grind.

CREDITS

Editor: Joshua Raab, joshuaraab.com

Cover Designer: DiztriX, 99designs.ca

Web Developer for TheGrind.gg: Nicky Hajal, nickyhajal.com

Proofreader& Consultant: Adam Morehouse, twitch.tv/novawar

Gaming peripherals of choice: Corsair, corsair.com

Back cover photographer: Josh LaTendresse, Insta @stormytheninja

20195244R00061

Made in the USA
Lexington, KY
03 December 2018